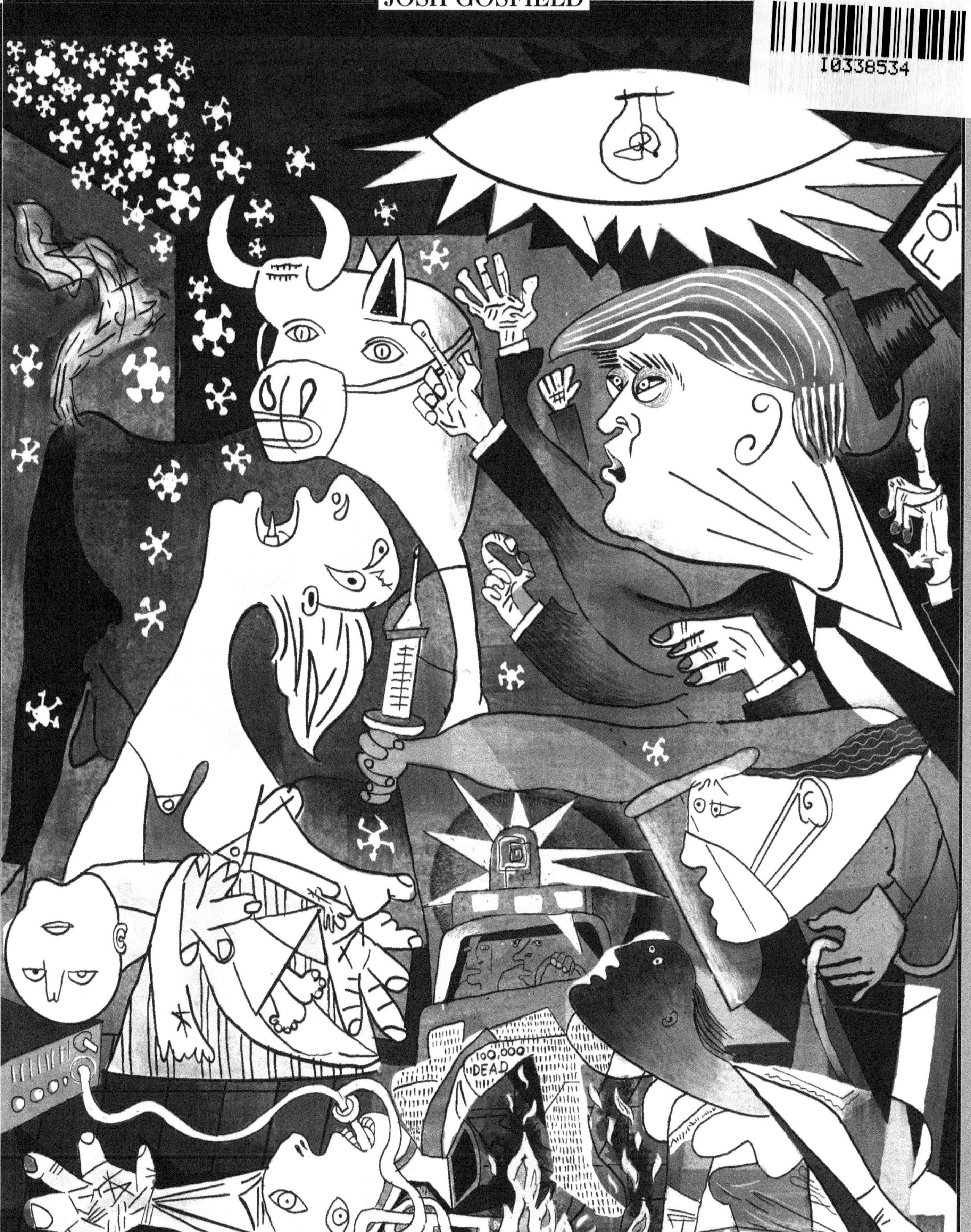
FOX
100,000
DEAD
Gosfield

"Coronica," June 2020.

BY MICHAEL GERBER

A LITTLE PATCH OF SUNSHINE

*The role of comedy when everything is well and truly f*cked*

When someone finds out I run a humor magazine, they always say the same thing: "Would you look at this mole on my neck?" (Apparently the acoustics are very poor.)

After I correct them, they say, "Trump, COVID, what great material! You must be psyched."

I'm not. Great comedy isn't usually produced by the truly awful; that's why there's no Jeeves and Wooster novel set at the Somme. *Jojo Rabbit* got exponentially less funny the more you knew about the real Berlin in 1945.

For comedy, things should be a bummer, not terrifying; herpes, yes—AIDS, no. COVID, for example, will only become "great material" after there's a vaccine. 2022 will be full of hilarious romantic comedies with masks as plot points. And three years after Trump dies, Armando Iannucci will remake *The Great Dictator*.

But now? All too terrible, too real, too close. I regret to inform you that if the USPS goes under, so does *Bystander*, along with every other newspaper and magazine that uses the mails—unless they get a special carve-out. Publishers will have to ask the government for a favor, and that favor will be granted, to some, for a very obvious price.

Our current era is no joke. Tyranny is easy, comedy is hard.

So if the Four Horsemen of the Apocalypse are no fun at parties, why invite them at all? Why even mention Trump or police brutality or coronavirus? Believe me, I've considered it; I could climb the rostrum (yes, we have one) and declare: "The purpose of *Bystander* is to be a respite, an island of gentle hilarity at the center of the hurricane. Now, for your enjoyment, here are 350 cartoons set in a psychiatrist's office."

I do a bit of that this ish (p. 50), and #16 will be tipped further towards Mindless Summer Fun. But, perhaps like you, my geniality conceals a slyly oppositional nature. If this really is a turning point in history, I'm determined to get in as many last licks as I can.

Speaking of history, there's another concern which matters a lot to the frustrated historian in me: Humor magazines are great *sources*. The topics they talk about, and how they talk about them, are an unfakeable look inside the noggins of people living at a certain time and place. The assumptions, the psychology…it's all laid bare. To draw a veil over what's going on in America at this crucial time would make us less intelligible to those who come after, and I couldn't live with that—as lucrative as it would be. Not for nothing do they say satire closes on a Saturday night.

In the U.S., satire's protected (for the moment), because it has a salutary effect; this effect comes from identifying real threats, and riling audiences up. Do I think satire saves lives? Not directly. That's a kind of comedy machismo that I just don't see reflected in the historical record. I agree with the English satirist Peter Cook, who once announced that he was starting a nightclub "in the spirit of those German cabarets that had done so much to prevent the rise of Hitler." That's on my gently manic days; on my gently depressed ones, I think of Cook's collaborator Jonathan Miller, who warned of the UK "sinking giggling into the sea," soothed by satire that only *felt* like action.*

So *Bystander*'s playing a double game—to entertain *and* bear witness—and is thus guaranteed to please no one. I know that, you know that. It's the joke at the core of this whole venture. As I was typing this, our cartoonist Nick Spooner texted to say that his brother-in-law, an intelligent and moral police officer, was enraged by the cartoon at left. I texted back, "Your broth-

Before

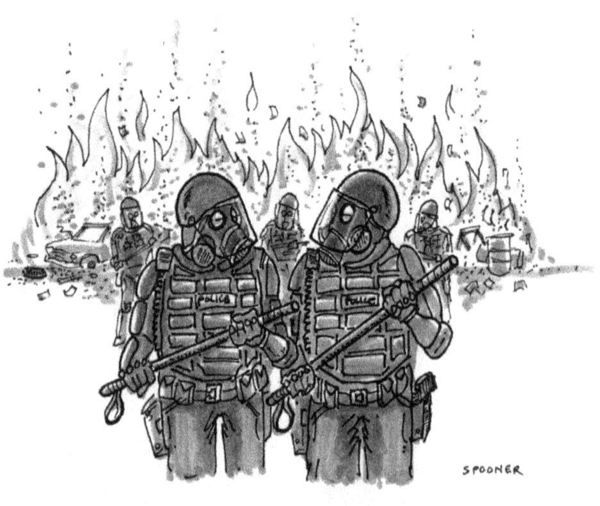
POLICE
POLICE
SPOONER

"And remember: their taxes pay our salaries."

*See also "The March to Restore Sanity and/or Fear," 10/30/2010.

er-in-law's rage is appropriate— not at a cartoonist's exaggeration, but at a world insane enough for people to recognize it in that cartoon." My heart breaks for the protesters, for Black Americans *and* for all of us warped by white supremacy. We're all, every one of us, including that cop, being fucked over by a bunch of history we didn't create—but we can reject it, and build something better.

To do that, though, we have to stay sane, and that's where the laughs come in. How do we somehow wring enough chuckles out of this harrowing time? I honestly don't know. I can only tell you what I'm doing: Nutshot videos.

In this blighted era, where basic freedoms—and even our shared humanity—is under organized assault, I'm going to YouTube and looking at guys getting booped in the balls. It's particularly hilarious slooowed down.

I wish I wasn't like this. I wish I was taking solace in, I dunno, the epigrams of Martial or something. My parents paid good money for me to become a person like that and I want to say right now to both of them: I'm sorry. It just didn't take. Have you seen the one where they use a two-by-four with a shoe on it? Jesus may have died for our sins, but that teenager gave, I think we can agree, so very much more.

If authoritarianism is going to fail in America (as it—please God!—appears it might), it won't have been vanquished through argument or force. It will have failed because of America's childish desire to do exactly what we want, when we want, and tell everyone else to go get fucked. Trump and his ilk use that against us, but comedy can channel it into a positive, by helping us live in truth. I'm an American; you can tell me anything, but you can't teach me anything. *You can't even stop me from Rube Goldberging my own 'nads.* But when I laughed at Dave Chappelle's "8:46," I taught myself: White supremacy is a punchline because it's *ridiculous*.

After

JONATHAN PLOTKIN

So what to do? Seek your own truth. Find your own patch of sunshine, and just *lay out*. Order that burrito. Glue sixty yards of Astroturf to your car. Find your kink; on Zoom, nobody knows you're wearing a nine-inch purple strap-on named "Percy." That's deeply antifa; if you don't believe me, tell someone even slightly Fa and see how they react.

Let Percy be our totem, our symbol. One of the strongest bulwarks against tyranny is unapologetically being yourself; others see that and do the same, and the herd anxiety at the heart of authoritarianism—and racism—dissipates. We're all weirdos. Our only safety is in numbers, and the only group big enough to protect all of us, is all of us.

I'm the last person to listen to; I run a print humor magazine. I can only say that my happiness has increased with my ability to figure out what is true, starting with the inside of me first. That's really what *Bystander* is all about; making something for people who are weird the same way I'm weird. We see a print humor magazine, of all things, and feel the warm glow of sunshine on the back of our neck.

(Wow. Now that I see it in the light? You should definitely get that mole checked out.) B

TABLE OF CONTENTS

DEPARTMENTS
"Coronica" *by Josh Gosfield* 1
Publisher's Letter *by Michael Gerber* 2
Rogues' Gallery: Brian McConnachie
   by B.A. Van Sise 76

QUARANTINE CAVALCADE
A collection of words and pictures produced between March and July 2020 by Melissa Balmain, Len Stokes, David Lancaster, Nathan Place, Adrian Bonenberger, Jessica Ziegler, Stan Mack, K.A. Polzin, Jonathan Zeller, Michael Pershan, D.J. Paris, Neil Shapiro, Lars Kenseth, and Victor Juhasz. 11

SHORT STUFF
A Guru'd Awakening
   by D. Watson 8
Happy Mother's Day!
   by Michael Gerber 19
Cowboy Dance Future World
   by Jack Handey 20
Lives of the Artist *by Kyle Berlin* 22
I'm Sorry Our First Heist Meeting
   Is On Zoom *by Meg Favreau* 24
Don't Re-Open Hogwarts!
   by Joe Janes (& Mike G.) 26
Please Take Me Down
   by Bronze Teddy Roosevelt 28

"The Trump Gang," by ZACHARY PULLEN

The AMERICAN BYSTANDER

#15 • Vol. 4, No. 3 • July 2020

EDITOR & PUBLISHER
Michael Gerber
HEAD WRITER
Brian McConnachie
SENIOR EDITOR
Alan Goldberg
ORACLE Steve Young
STAFF LIAR P.S. Mueller
INTREPID TRAVELER Mike Reiss
EAGLE EYES Patrick L. Kennedy
AGENTS OF THE SECOND BYSTANDER INTERNATIONAL
Eve Alintuck, Craig Boreth, Joey Green, Matt Kowalick, Neil Mitchell, Maxwell Ziegler
MANAGING EDITOR EMERITA
Jennifer Finney Boylan
WARTIME CONSIGLIERA
Kate Powers
CONTRIBUTORS
Melissa Balmain, Nat Benchley, Tracey Berglund, Kyle Berlin, Barry Blitt, Adrian Bonenberger, George Booth, T.Q. Chen, Tyson Cole, Joe Dottino, Marques Duggans, Ivan Ehlers, Meg Favreau, Rick Geary, Josh Gosfield, Sam Gross, Jack Handey, Joe Janes, Ted Jouflas, Victor Juhasz, Lars Kenseth, Peter Kuper, David Lancaster, Ross MacDonald, Stan Mack, Tim O'Brien, D.J. Paris, Michael Pershan, Nathan Place, Jonathan Plotkin, K.A. Polzin, Zachary Pullen, Marc Rosenthal, Arnold Roth, Cris Shapan, Neil Shapiro, Jim Siergey, Greg Simetz, Nick Spooner, Len Stokes, Ed Subitzky, B.A. Van Sise, Dalton Vaughn, D. Watson, Cerise Zelenetz, Jonathan Zeller, Jessica Ziegler.

Caroline Roth, Lanky Bareikis, Jon Schwarz, Karen Backus, Alleen Schultz, Diane Gray, Molly Bernstein, Joe Lopez, Eliot Ivanhoe, Neil Gumenick, Greg and Patricia Gerber and many others.
NAMEPLATES BY Mark Simonson
ISSUE CREATED BY Michael Gerber

Vol. 4, No. 3. ©2020 Good Cheer LLC, all rights reserved. Proudly produced in sunny Santa Monica, California, USA.

FEATURES

Baseball in the Time of COVID-19 *by Jim Siergey & Greg Simetz*	31
Little Donald's Sneeze *by Peter Kuper*	34
Window Portraits *by B.A. Van Sise*	35
Fred's Day *by Ed Subitzky*	43
COVID-19 Expeditionary Force *by Marc Rosenthal*	44
The Assassin *by Jennifer Finney Boylan*	46
A Guide to Masked Emotions, Volume 1 *by Nick Spooner*	55
Les Dents de la Mer *by Nat Benchley*	56
T.Q. Chen's Quarantine Diary *by Tianqi Chen*	59
Quarantine Queen *by Ted Jouflas*	65

OUR BACK PAGES
Notes From a Small Planet *by Rick Geary* 71
What Am I Doing Here? *by Mike Reiss* 73
P.S. Mueller Thinks Like This *by P.S. Mueller* 75

CARTOONS & ILLUSTRATIONS BY
Harry Bliss, Josh Gosfield, Zachary Pullen, George Booth, Barry Blitt, Ross MacDonald, Sam Gross, D. Watson, Len Stokes, Nathan Place, Stan Mack, K.A. Polzin, Neil Shapiro, Victor Juhasz, Ivan Ehlers, Marques Duggans, Dalton Vaughn, Peter Kuper, Cerise Zelenetz, Joe Dottino, Tyson Cole, Tracey Berglund, Arnold Roth, and P.S. Mueller.

Sam's Spot

COVER

When the miraculous **HARRY BLISS** suggested this cover idea, I immediately thought of it as the second part of a matched set. Paired with #14's cover by **JOHN CUNEO**, it shows before and after, pre-COVID and post-, old reality and new. Someday the masks will come off, and the kissing can recommence. But in the meantime, we take deep breaths and envy our dogs their sweet, suddenly not-so-simple pleasures. Thanks, Harry—been wanting you on the cover of *Bystander* for years. And you're right: you *do* draw a great tree.

ACKNOWLEDGMENTS

All material is ©2020 its creators, all rights reserved; please do not reproduce or distribute it without written consent of the creators and *The American Bystander*. The following material has previously appeared, and is reprinted here with permission of the author(s): P.S. Mueller's "The Blight Stuff" first appeared in *Rosebud Magazine*.

THE AMERICAN BYSTANDER, Vol. 4, No. 3, (978-0-57-871533-9). Publishes ~4x/year. ©2020 by Good Cheer LLC. No part of this magazine can be reproduced, in whole or in part, by any means, without the written permission of the Publisher. For this and other queries, email *Publisher@americanbystander.org*, or write: Michael Gerber, Publisher, *The American Bystander*, 1122 Sixth St., #403, Santa Monica, CA 90403. **Subscribe at www.patreon.com/bystander.** More—perhaps too much—information can be found on the web at www.americanbystander.org.

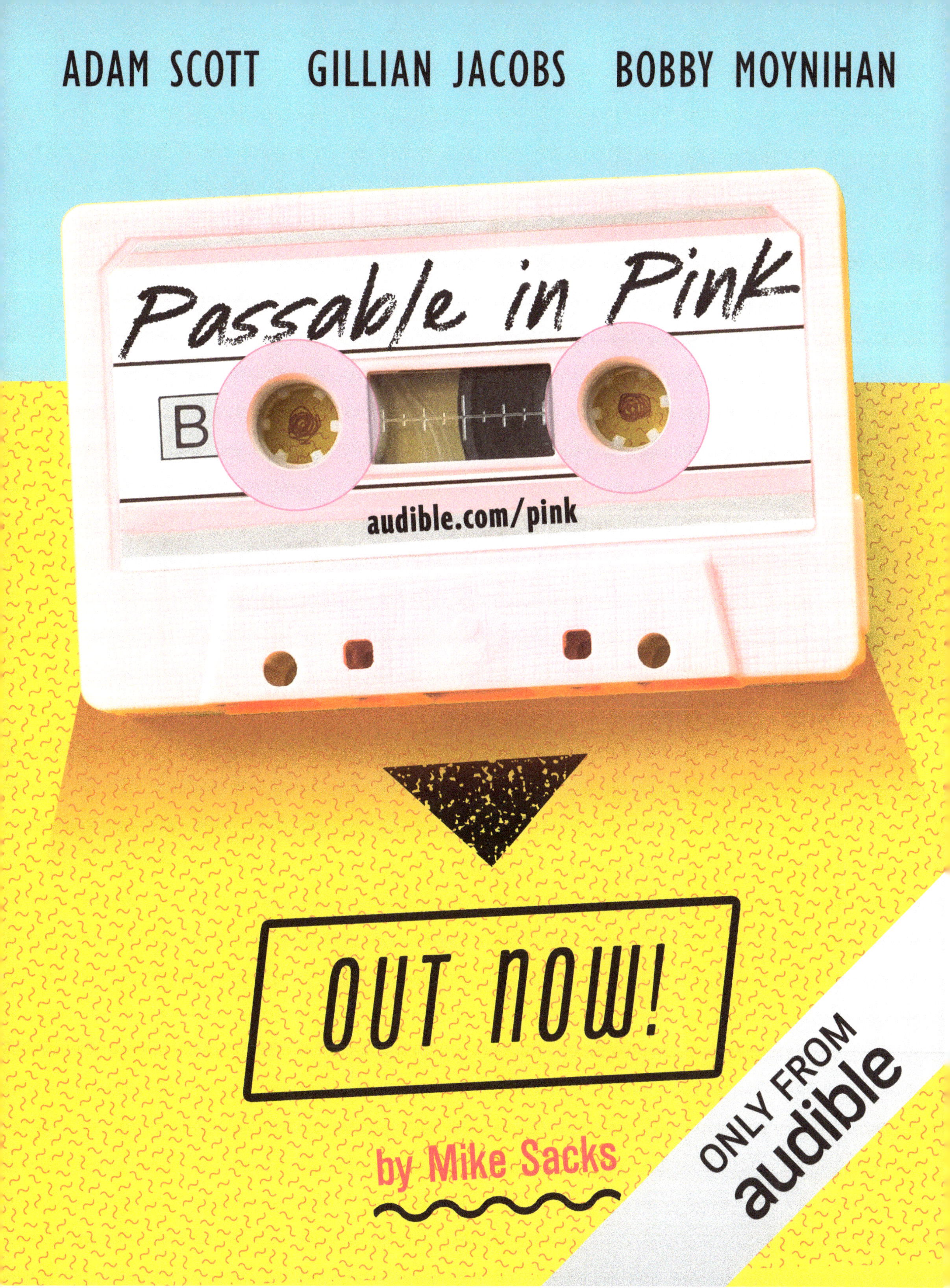

ADAM SCOTT GILLIAN JACOBS BOBBY MOYNIHAN
Passable in Pink
B
audible.com/pink
OUT NOW!
by Mike Sacks
ONLY FROM
audible

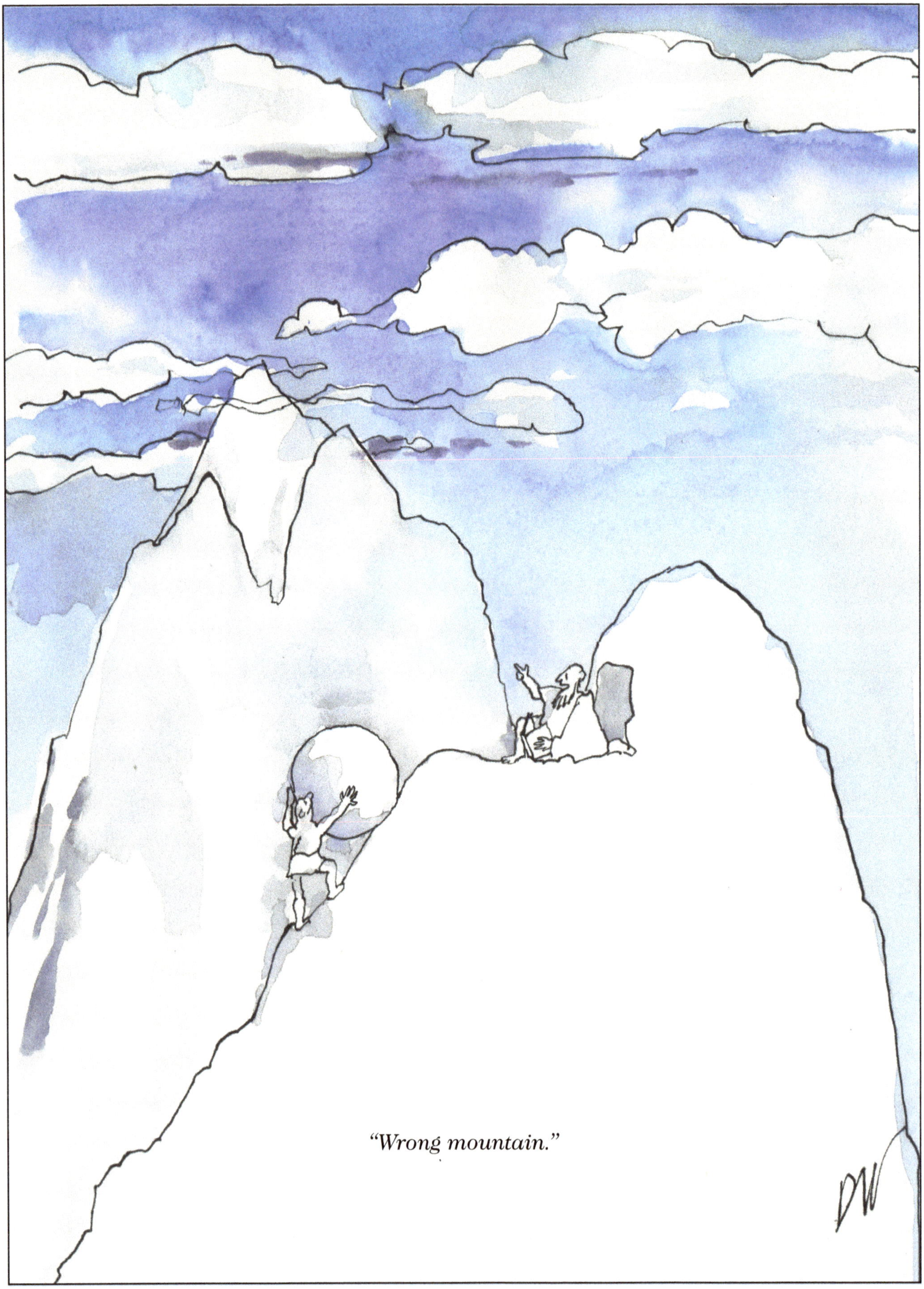
DW

"Wrong mountain."

… EARIOS

THE MARGARET CHO

ICONIC COMEDIAN MARGARET CHO TALKS WITH PEOPLE YOU KNOW, AND PEOPLE YOU SHOULD KNOW.

  acast

COMING APRIL 2020 FROM FANTAGRAPHICS BOOKS

The art of B.K. Taylor, ripped from the pages of *National Lampoon*:

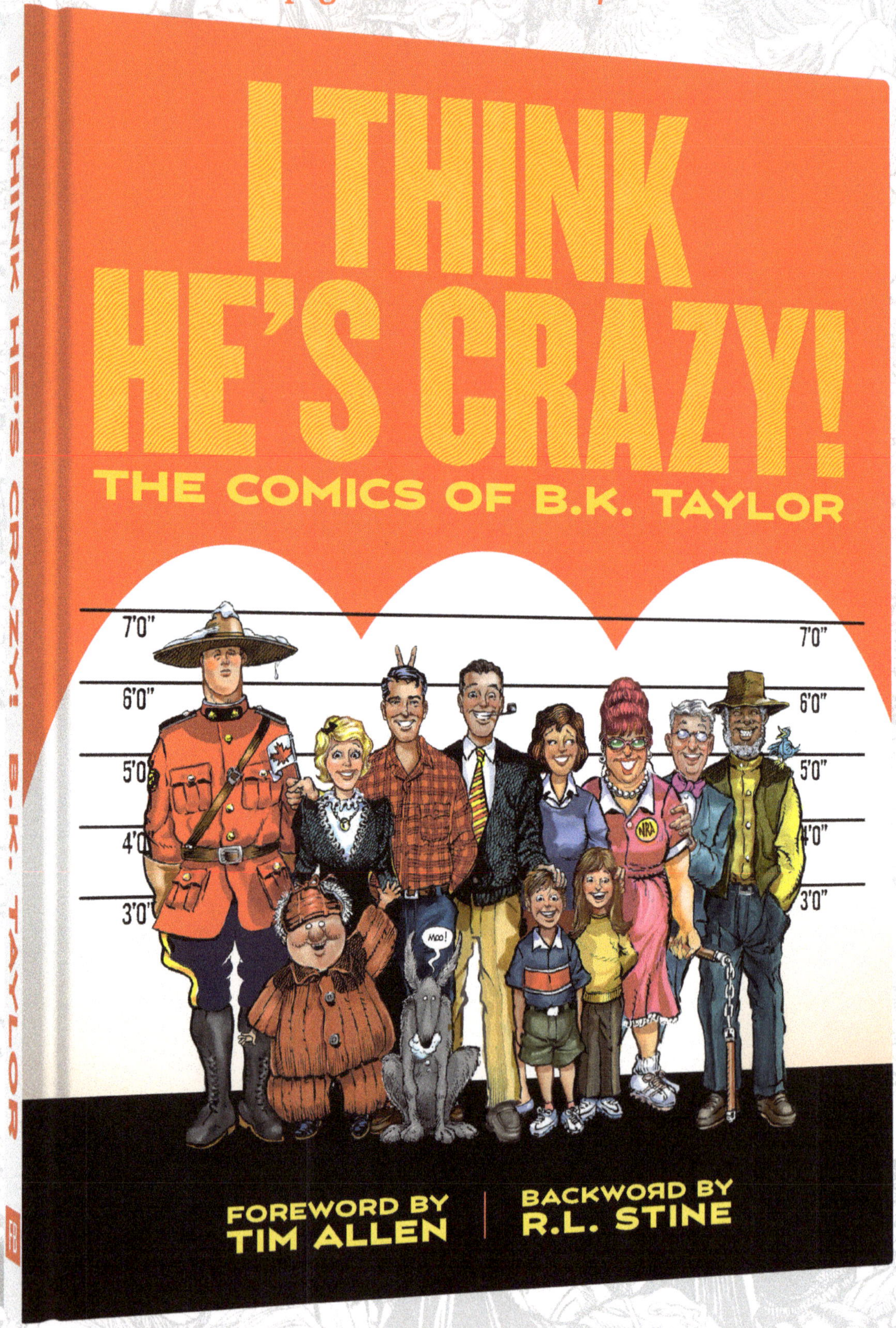

I THINK HE'S CRAZY!
THE COMICS OF B.K. TAYLOR

FOREWORD BY **TIM ALLEN** | BACKWORD BY **R.L. STINE**

Exclusive offer for *American Bystander* readers: Order this book from the Fantagraphics website and use the promo code BYSTANDER to get 20% off!

FANTAGRAPHICS.COM/BK-TAYLOR

Quarantine Cavalcade

"Crazy, man, crazy."

WHEN THE CHIPS ARE DOWN...

Is your pulsating earache a thing-you-
  should-fear ache?
Could tumors be lodged in your brain?
Do you let this one slide or risk taking
  a ride
to a clinic? Your choice becomes plain:
you'll stay in, drink some gin, picture
  numbers that spin,
place your bet...
and start playing pandemic roulette.

Now your cat's acting grumpy, and
  smells like some lump he
coughed up on the living room
  floor—
should you grab him and go for
  a checkup, or no?
You decide that you'll have to
  ignore
the new whir in his purr and
  the mats in his fur,
skip the vet,
and keep playing pandemic
  roulette.

Plus of course there's your
  toddler, that balance-free
  waddler,
and clumsy, impetuous spouse:
when they topple and bleed, is
  a pro what they need?
Nah, you'll stitch them up right
  in the house,
getting by, while they cry, with
  some tips from a guy
on the Net,
since you're playing pandemic
  roulette.

It's the closest to Vegas you'll come in
  this plague, as
you gamble no torment or ill
(that you'd normally shout to a doctor
  about)
will deform or disable or kill
while you wait and you wait for that
  mythical date
when the threat
is no sweat
and you'll get—
you hope yet!—
to quit playing pandemic roulette.
—Melissa Balmain

LEN STOKES

MY COVID DIARY.

6:00 am: Thought about getting up, then remembered I have absolutely no reason to live. So: slept in!

9:02 am: Is this a pastries-made-with-lard day or a pastries-made-with-butter day? Consulted yesterday's entry. Thank God. *Lard.*

10:05 am: Pondered which of my pets would devour my COVID-ravaged corpse. Whispered to the cat, "Eat me and you'll get it."

11:30 am: Managed to hack the Supreme Court conference call while taking a dump.

1:28 pm: Finished naming blades of grass in northeast quadrant...Betsy DeVos, Lil Yachty, Cantinflas. Wait, there you are, Ramón! Thought I'd never see you again.

2:00 pm: Arranged spices by country of origin.

3:45 pm: Rearranged them by personality.

4:50 pm: Looked up more cool projects on Sisyphus.com.

5:00 pm: Took copious notes at the President's coronavirus press briefing, then fact-checked them on Breitbart. All good.

6:30 pm: Examined paint samples for dining room. Tried to cover for the fact that I cannot tell "Scottish Moss" from "Misty Sage." (Think my wife suspects.)

8:15 pm: Tried to remember

anything between 6:00 am and 8:15 pm. Couldn't.
8:45 pm: Decided to learn a new language on Duolingo. I'm thinking ancient Greek. Make that Latin. Pig Latin.
9:15 pm: Mental note: kill the next person who says, "We're all in this together."
10:00 pm: Read and re-read the beloved parts of the Bible that encourage slavery.
11:00 pm: Turned in with a delicious bedtime cocktail, the Don Collins (gin, club soda, lemon-scented Lysol). Noticed my pets are…drooling?

—David Lancaster

SEVEN WAYS TO MANAGE YOUR ANXIETY ABOUT HOW TO MANAGE YOUR CORONAVIRUS ANXIETY.

There's a lot of anxiety around coronavirus and the associated quarantine. Luckily, many people and groups are stepping up to help. Unfortunately, the proliferation of advice from various medical institutions competing for influence can itself be a source of anxiety. Below are seven ways to manage your anxiety about evaluating sources of guidance and tips about coronavirus-related anxiety.

Don't pay attention to the number of tips offered in a given story. Let's be honest, there aren't that many things one can do to actually manage one's stress over a worldwide pandemic. If a story purports to offer more than nine pieces of advice, chances are it's just going to end up making you more anxious. Accept no more than nine ways to manage your stress per article about managing stress—seven's better, of course (and three is probably best).

Read one article at a time. It will be tempting to open as many different pieces as you can and read them simultaneously. This is a mistake! The human brain can only process one thing at a time. Focus on reading a single piece about managing your anxiety about coronavirus or the quarantine, or you will definitely become increasingly anxious. This is natural—you are actually overwhelming yourself. Just read one at a time!

It's not a competition. Sure, your friend already knows a thousand tips for managing anxiety stemming from coronavirus aka COVID-19. Good for them! You don't need to make an exhaustive labor out of tracking down every piece of advice from every medical institution, then delve into (heaven forbid) personal blogs in a desperate attempt to "beat" your friend by knowing more about this terrifying and unprecedented situation. Just thinking about it is making me anxious, so I'm going to stop. You should too! Limit yourself to a few general guidelines and maybe an anecdote or two—enough to have a conversation over the phone, but not so exhaustive that you end up driving yourself nuts. You'll end up driving other people nuts, too. Like your spouse.

Call a divorce lawyer. Okay, now is not the time to panic, but... your neurotic obsession with managing your anxiety around coronavirus aka COVID-19 and the quarantine is almost certainly rubbing off on your spouse. They're not sick of you yet, but you can see where this is headed, 12 hours into a pandemic that's sure to last weeks or even months. Your buddy knows a guy who did divorce law in Louisiana for a while. He should know someone. Someone to figure out what the damage will be if your spouse decides that your encyclopedic knowledge of how to manage your anxious feelings is grounds for permanent separation.

Plot the perfect crime. The divorce lawyer hung up on you after just a few minutes, and you could hear your spouse's phone ringing right after that. They were certain that you'd gone "totally off the deep end with this coronavirus stuff," and now they want to encourage your spouse to leave you. There's only one thing to do: plan and execute the perfect crime.

First, turn on the gas stove; then, call

A DAY IN THE LIFE OF THE "ALL LIVES MATTER" GUY
HAPPY BIRTHDAY TO EVERYONE.
GOD BLESS ALL COUNTRIES.
GO BOTH TEAMS.
SPORTS
TIGERS
#1
TIGERS!
HELP ME!!
HELP US ALL.
NPLACE

your eccentric neighbor, who is a heavy smoker and chocaholic. Tell him your spouse made some delicious brownies, and that you have left a plate of them in the kitchen. Then drive over to your friend's house for an alibi. Tell him you need some tips on how to battle anxiety regarding coronavirus aka COVID-19 and the quarantine.

His nose dulled by years of Kools, your neighbor will smell nothing. Frustrated by his inability to find brownies which are not there, he will light up. The fireball will be seen for miles.

My god, what have you done. There's no going back now. You need to get to Canada, and fast. Hit a couple stores for a gun and ammo, and make your way north using back roads. Stay away from highways, and steal some new license plates; they'll have your name out on an APB for sure. When you get close to the border, ditch the car and find a place to cross on foot. You can't think about the past. Now, you must think about the future.

You made it! But what's that cough? You're free! Nobody can stop you now, the idiots in the police were too busy dealing with the quarantine to even question you! But somehow you seem to have picked up a cough and a low-grade fever—maybe from the gun store? It was probably that guy behind the counter wearing a clever T-shirt about vaccines being a conspiracy. Damn it! After all that, you still got coronavirus aka COVID-19!!!! Time to make your way to the Internet and figure out what to do next...

—Adrian Bonenberger

THINGS THAT MIGHT TREAT CORONAVIRUS.

• Swallowing 4 AAA batteries
• Shining a laser pointer directly into your eye
• Shoving a Flaming Hot Cheeto up each nostril (really cram it in there)
• Several "Coronabombs": a shot of gasoline dropped in a Bud Light, chugged
• Soaking in the fresh tears of local Democrats
• Slathering yourself in a slurry of Softscrub and coconut oil, then sitting in direct sunlight for 6-7 hours
• A jalapeño slice taped to each nipple
• Actual ants in your pants. And by "pants" I mean underwear, and by "ants" I mean fire ants.
• Listerine eye wash

Why not try it? What have you got to lose? I'll say it again...whathaveyougottolose?? Try it. If you want. — *The CDC.*

—Jessica Ziegler

STAN MACK'S CHRONICLES

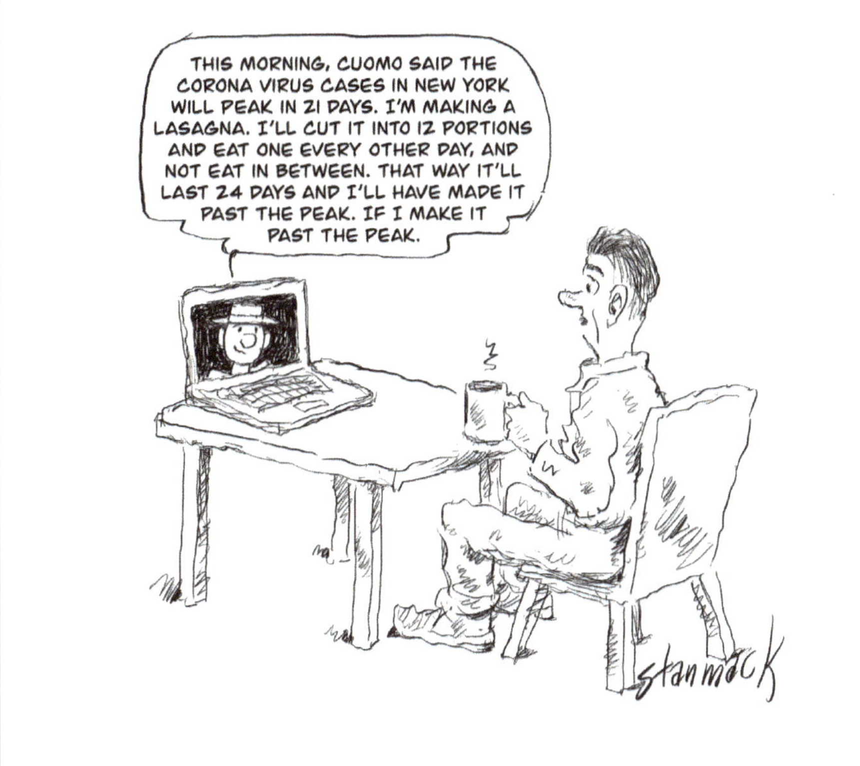
THIS MORNING, CUOMO SAID THE CORONA VIRUS CASES IN NEW YORK WILL PEAK IN 21 DAYS. I'M MAKING A LASAGNA. I'LL CUT IT INTO 12 PORTIONS AND EAT ONE EVERY OTHER DAY, AND NOT EAT IN BETWEEN. THAT WAY IT'LL LAST 24 DAYS AND I'LL HAVE MADE IT PAST THE PEAK. IF I MAKE IT PAST THE PEAK.
stanmack

IT'S HARD TO MAKE FRIENDS AS AN ADULT, BECAUSE YOU'RE NOT ALLOWED TO GO OUTSIDE OR DO ANYTHING.

When I was younger, it felt like I made friends everywhere I went. But now, as an adult, it's much more difficult. I think the main problem is that we're not allowed to go anywhere or do anything.

It was simpler when we were kids, and it wasn't dangerous to get within six feet of another person.

Do you remember when you were in elementary school, and any other child who liked the same baseball team, video game, or TV show as you was a pal? And you could walk up to him, and if you shared his toy truck you didn't think it would lead to your death or the death of a loved one because it contained an invisible army of germs that you would accidentally put in your nose, mouth, or eyes?

Now we're older. We're busy working from home all day, getting sore backs from hunching over our laptops at an awkward angle. We're worried that we're running out of canned soup and seltzer, and scared to go to the store to get more. Every surface is teeming with tiny enemies waiting to destroy us. With all that to occupy us, it's no wonder that we don't have time to meet anyone new.

And even if we encounter someone else with whom we seem compatible for friendship—perhaps a guy in a Jimmy Eat World T-shirt we see standing across the way as we stroll through the park with our dog—we know that the risk of standing close enough to have a conversation is too great.

When he comes near, we scream "SOCIAL DISTANCING!" If he reaches for our dog, we lift the dog into our arms and stumble back at least six feet, as fast

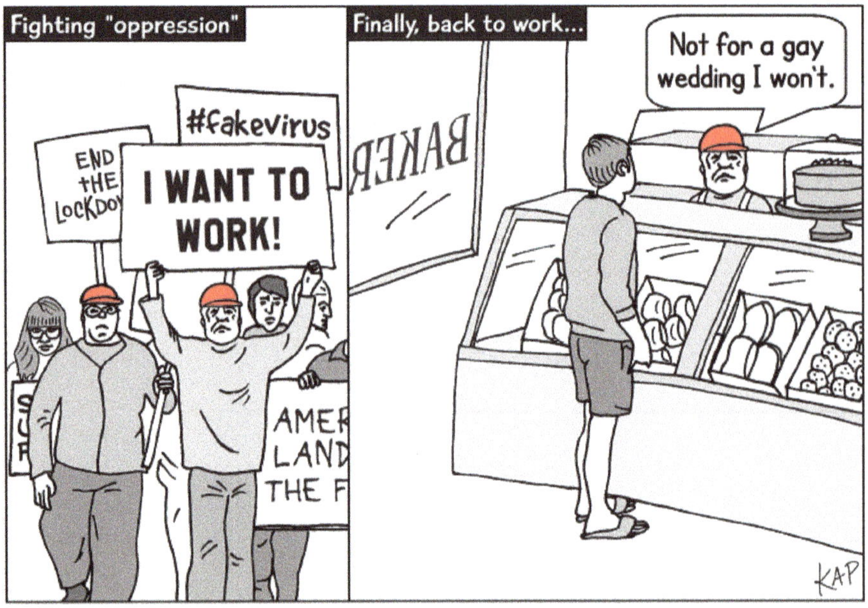
Fighting "oppression"
#fakevirus
END THE LOCKDO
I WANT TO WORK!
AMER LAND THE F
Finally, back to work...
Not for a gay wedding I won't.
KAP

as we can. Because human interaction has become poison.

There's no denying that it's tough to make friends as an adult. But that doesn't mean it's not worth trying. Every once in a while, you have to get out there in a full hazmat suit, making sure no part of you is exposed to the air, stand across the street from a stranger, and shout "*Hello! What are your interests?*"

And if it turns out you have a lot in common—like both of you have cracked, bleeding hands from incessant hand-washing yet live in terror that you've made a small, careless mistake that will lead to your demise—and he invites you to go do something fun, do not take your phone out to record his number. Your phone is the dirtiest thing you own. Have him scream his number to you, and repeat it back to him. Memorization is the most sanitary way to file someone's contact information.

Do not go with your new friend to a second location, no matter how enthusiastic he may be, and do not approach to shake hands or get a clearer view of his face. Let it remain a blur buried deep in your mind, like the fading memory of everything you took for granted in February.

—Jonathan Zeller

PHARAOH SPEAKS OUT ABOUT THE UPCOMING TENTH PLAGUE.

My fellow Egyptians—Like many of us, I worry about this so-called "tenth plague." Early indications suggest it will primarily target the firstborn. Thankfully, I am not in this high-risk group—but even those of us not at risk for the plague must be vigilant. We must take steps to protect the most vulnerable members of our society.

I mean, of course, the Israelite slaves.

There is much we don't know about the plague, but court magicians suspect Israelites will be uniquely prone to it. The slaves live in shoddy mud huts in crowded slums. Due to their weak physical constitutions, they frequently complain about even minor ailments. And because of their belief in YHWH, they lack the protective amulets that are the backbone of the famous Egyptian healthcare system.

So this plague could hit the Israelites hard. Over the past few days, Egyptians have been obeying strict isolation orders. Israelites, on the other hand, are preparing for some sort of large family gathering involving a sheep, crackers and cheap wine. The plague will doubtless find an easy target in the Israelites at these gatherings, given their many digestive problems. Egypt is ready for the plague, but are the Israelites?

To make things worse, these Israelites are arrogant. They seem to think a bit of blood on the doorpost will keep them safe. But, as the latest magical research shows, blood on the doorpost attracts the plague, rather than repelling it. The Israelites will suffer for their superstitious beliefs. Yep, this is what you get for underinvesting in polytheism.

I'm calling for immediate action. Pharaoh's office needs to massively ramp up their production of amulets. But amulets won't be enough; we'll also need trinkets. If we can get enough amulets and trinkets to protect the Israelites, we might just get through this thing.

These will be a difficult few days for all Egyptians. But don't forget about our most vulnerable people. Because if we don't protect them now, we might have to start imagining life in Egypt without them.

—Michael Pershan

NOW THAT I CAN'T GO ANYWHERE, I DON'T FEEL GUILTY ABOUT NOT GOING ANYWHERE.

I would love to tell you that my life has significantly changed since the stay-at-home order. I would also love to tell you that I have six-pack abs and that I'm president of MENSA. But I would be lying. And while lying has served me well over the years, I feel it's time to come clean.

The reality is that coronavirus hasn't changed my life at all. Not one itty bitty bit.

Let's start with the whole going outside thing. I never did that. I mean, once in a while if there was a parade and the route went right by my place and all I had to do was step onto my porch to wave at the floats—okay, then I'd go out. Or if I needed to get cat litter, sure. I'd drive to the litter store. But mostly I stay inside. I have video games and streaming services and food delivery. That stuff alone occupies 90% of my waking hours.

What about when I want to spend time in nature? Well, that's what windows are for! The Chicago River is right outside my apartment, and I stare at it every day. From my couch. I can even see the water surface rippling if I squint. One time I walked outside down to the riverbank to make sure I wasn't missing anything. Nope—exactly the same. Only with mosquitos.

Even though I've made a comfortable life for myself throughout the years, I always felt that I should be exploring life outside these condo walls. Why am I watching the series finale of *M*A*S*H* for the seventh time instead of, say, visiting a museum? Actually… museums suck. Not a good example. But you understand my point. I should have been out exploring.

However, something has changed in my life since COVID-19 arrived. A significant change so profound and unexpected that I shared it with my therapist yesterday. During my revelation Zoom froze and we got disconnected, but I'm pretty sure she heard me. I was telling her that all of my previous guilt and shame for not leaving the house has now been utterly extinguished.

Why the sudden leap in my self-esteem? Because now I'm just like you! For the first time in my forty-three years, the rest of you bozos are just as inactive as me. And while you might be going stir-crazy, I'm content staying in. I've had years of training. This is my lane, and I stay in it.

I guess what I'm saying is thank you. I'm grateful to finally be normal. Well, at least until this whole thing blows over and you're back to your regular life. That's gonna suck for me.

—D.J. Paris

THE BLOCK DOCTRINE.

"For thirty-five years, what has animated Friedman's counterrevolution is an attraction to the kind of freedom and possibility available only in times of cataclysmic change—when people, with their stubborn habits and insistent demands, are blasted out of the way—moments when democracy seems a practical impossibility."—Naomi Klein, ***The Shock Doctrine: The Rise of Disaster Capitalism***

Wake up. We are in serious trouble… and not in the way you think. While you and I sew cloth masks and can kumquats, our democracy is teetering on the brink of collapse. Opportunists and charlatans the world over have been waiting for this—a moment of pure chaos that they can leverage for their own personal benefit. Terry from next door is using a leaf blower, even though Santa Monica banned them years ago.

Powerful people are meeting in smoke-filled Zooms, not to reduce suffering, but to capitalize on it. Demoralizing, isn't it? Times of crisis should bring out the best in us, but for every honest broker there are twelve Sheilas from Apartment 8 who, for some reason, think they can just take any spot in the garage now. I'll be honest, it keeps me up at night.

Because it's not just a question of the rights we lose, it's also the rights we give away. Oh sure, someone always argues that it's for the greater good. That all you relinquish will be restored later, once the worst is over. But do you seriously believe Gretchen is going to return our loaf pan once August rolls around? I have my doubts.

That's not to say that we shouldn't make sacrifices. Now is the time to stand up, roll up our sleeves and sit down for ESPN's eight hours of trick-shot pool tournaments. I get it. But what I don't get is why the landscapers are only coming every other week. They usually wear masks anyway. At least when they do the weed cutter thing.

When will this tyranny end? Past may prove to be prologue. In 1973, CIA false-flag operations brought Pinochet to power. In 2004, the tsunami that crippled Sri Lanka prompted foreign investors to snap up coastline before the locals could rebuild. And ten minutes ago, those idiot

NEIL SHAPIRO

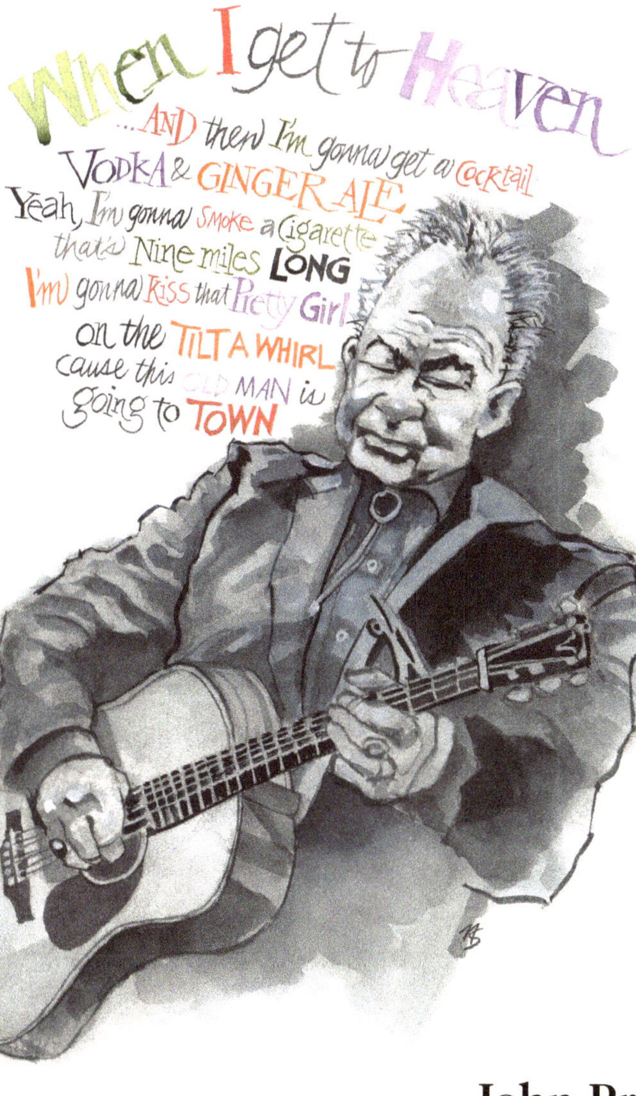
When I get to Heaven
...AND then I'm gonna get a cocktail
VODKA & GINGER ALE
Yeah, I'm gonna smoke a cigarette
that's Nine miles LONG
I'm gonna Kiss that Pretty Girl
on the TILT A WHIRL
cause this OLD MAN is
going to TOWN

John Prine
1946-2020

kids from two doors down decided to play football in the middle of the street. The ball hit my car. Or at least it could have.

The only way to stop exploitation like this is to call it out—but often the general public doesn't know the full extent of the wrongdoing until it's too late. This morning, Garrett who used to live below us posted a selfie…wearing my mirrored aviators. Garrett moved out September 15th, 2008, the day Lehman Brothers collapsed, plunging the country into the biggest financial crisis since the Great Depression. Coincidence? I think not.

My aim isn't to turn your quilting project into a patchwork Kleenex sopping with tears. I believe we have reason to hope—the knife of opportunism cuts both ways. Just as some bad actors use moments of chaos to enrich themselves, so too can we use them to promote positive change. If we can be vigilant, stay informed and find a way to come together, united against the robber-barons of our time, a better world is possible. I stole Terry's leaf blower and threw it in the trash.

—Lars Kenseth

HOW TO TELL IF YOU'VE GOT CORONAVIRUS.

Many people are unclear about the specific symptoms associated with coronavirus, or COVID-19, and even if they had the virus, they wouldn't know what to do about it. We reached out to Echo Crumb, "MD," medical and spiritual pseudoscientific expert, to help answer some of the biggest questions about the virus.

What is coronavirus?

First of all, a virus is basically a "bug," which is why people will say "I caught a bug," or "a bug is going around." How would you treat a bug you found in your home? You would slap it with your palm, or beneath a boot. Now obviously it is impractical to, say, surgically open a person's lungs and then just squish all the coronavirus bugs in the lung by slapping them or stomping them. We can all agree that such a notion is totally absurd! What we can do, if we have coronavirus or are afraid we have coronavirus, is accelerate and decelerate rapidly, such as… precisely! In a car, starting and stopping very abruptly (an accident, say).

What are the symptoms?

Symptoms of coronavirus include a fever, coughing, not being able to smell or taste, and not being able to breathe. The first thing you'll want to do if you're wondering if you have coronavirus instead of, say, the flu (very similar), or are in a *Langoliers*-style parallel dimension where time has stopped (the loss of smell and taste), or are drowning in the ocean or a lake (can't breathe), is assess one's surroundings. If one doesn't have the flu, is on dry land, and isn't in a terrifying Stephen King-penned nightmare scenario, then my friend: you have coronavirus.

How you can tell if someone you're talking to has coronavirus.

There's a lot of racism-driven fear about coronavirus, and we'd like to be the first to dispel rumors that any Chinese or Italian person has this disease. Okay? That's a scurrilous lie, intended to deflect attention from the people (?) who are truly responsible for the disease. I'm talking of course about the Langoliers. If you're talking to a Langolier, not only do they have the disease, the disease is their fault! I want to underline here that this isn't racism, it's nationalism, which is a very different and okay kind of prejudice to have.

I definitely have coronavirus, aka COVID-19. Now what?

This is very important. If you don't have a car to accelerate and then crash in, there's a small chance you'll get better, and a big chance you'll get worse. Do you really want to die in a hospital bed, surrounded by pretentious assholes telling you to breathe and trying to do surgery on your lungs to get at the bugs infesting them? No! You want to go down a hero, like Brünhilde in *Der Ring Des Nibelungen*! Whatever that means to you. Go be Brünhilde!

But what about social distancing?

As someone who's been practicing social distancing most of my life—you can't see or smell me right now, but if you could, you'd know why!—I think social distancing is always a good idea. The real question is, can you have too much of a good thing? Probably! Only time and science will tell.

I'm also terrified about the economy.

Buddy, listen, I hear you. My grandfather came over to America after Germany's economy was ruined in WWI, and he told my dad, Echo Sr., "Son, in America, even the dumbest guy with tiny hands can be president." I think about that a lot, now. Like, did my grandfather have prophetic powers? There's a lot we still don't know about the brain, it's a powerful thing. Anyway, I don't know too much about the economy, but I do have a diverse portfolio, about a year's worth of rice in my basement, and a pump-action 12-gauge shotgun, so ultimately I'm not too worried about it.

—Adrian Bonenberger **B**

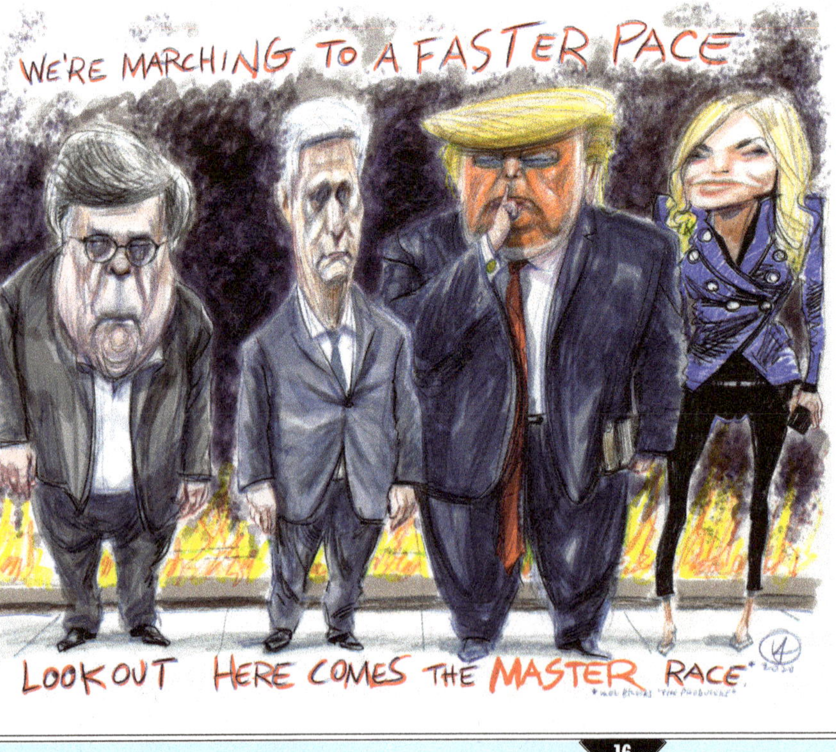
WE'RE MARCHING TO A FASTER PACE
LOOK OUT HERE COMES THE MASTER RACE*

DO YOU KNOW GINGER?

WE DO.

Created as the perfect conclusion to a great meal, Barrow's Intense is a cold pressed ginger liqueur, handcrafted in Brooklyn using more than 200lbs of fresh ginger per batch. Serve it over ice or add it to your favorite cocktail.

44 proof/22% ALC/VOL
Gluten Free, Vegan, Kosher (K)

★★★★
4 Stars/Highly Recommended & Superb
F. Paul Pacult / Spirit Journal Sept 2014

A+
Good Spirits News

2014 CRAFT SPIRITS AWARDS GOLD

94 THE TASTING PANEL

"Best in Class"
SIP AWARDS 2013 PLATINUM

BARROW'S
BARROW'S
BARROW'S
INTENSE
GINGER
LIQUEUR
HANDMADE IN BROOKLYN
Handmade in Brooklyn
750 ML
22% Alc/Vol (44 Proof)

barrowsintense.com

@barrowsintense

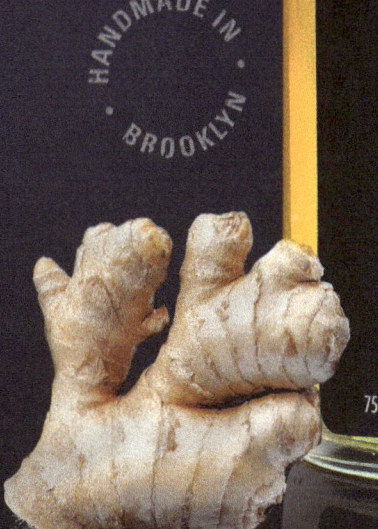

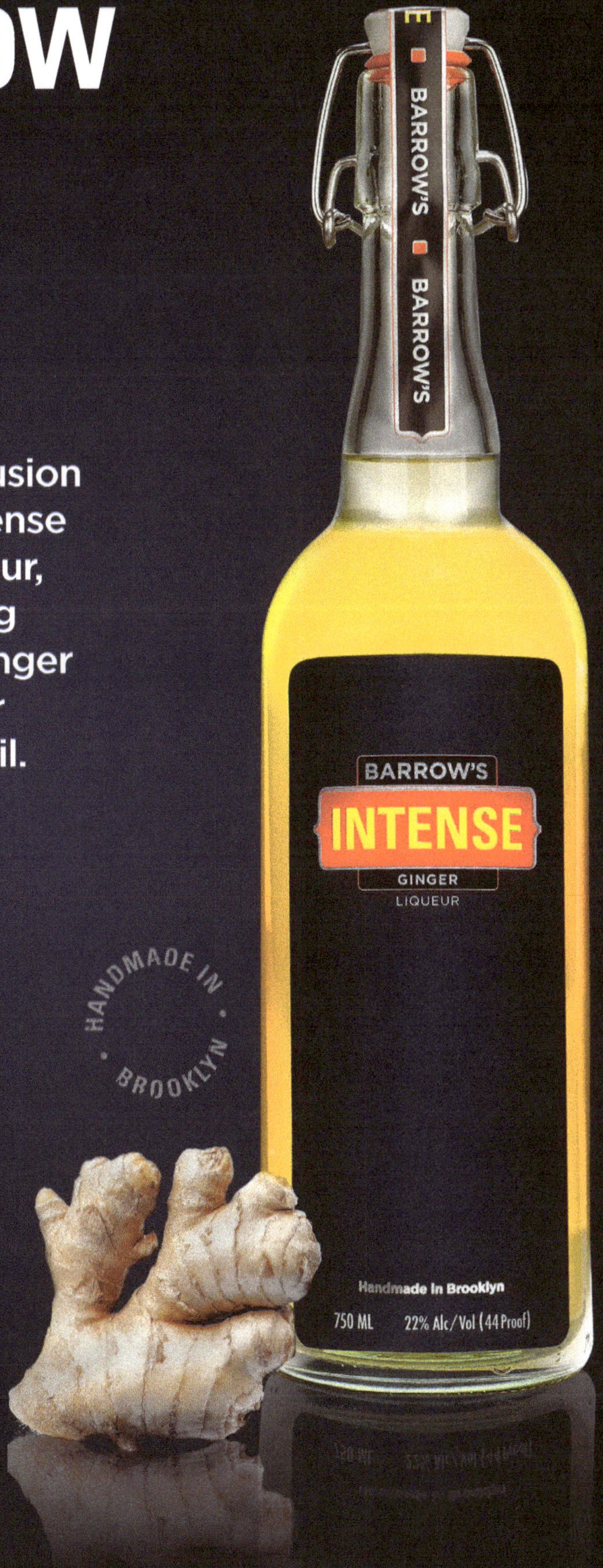

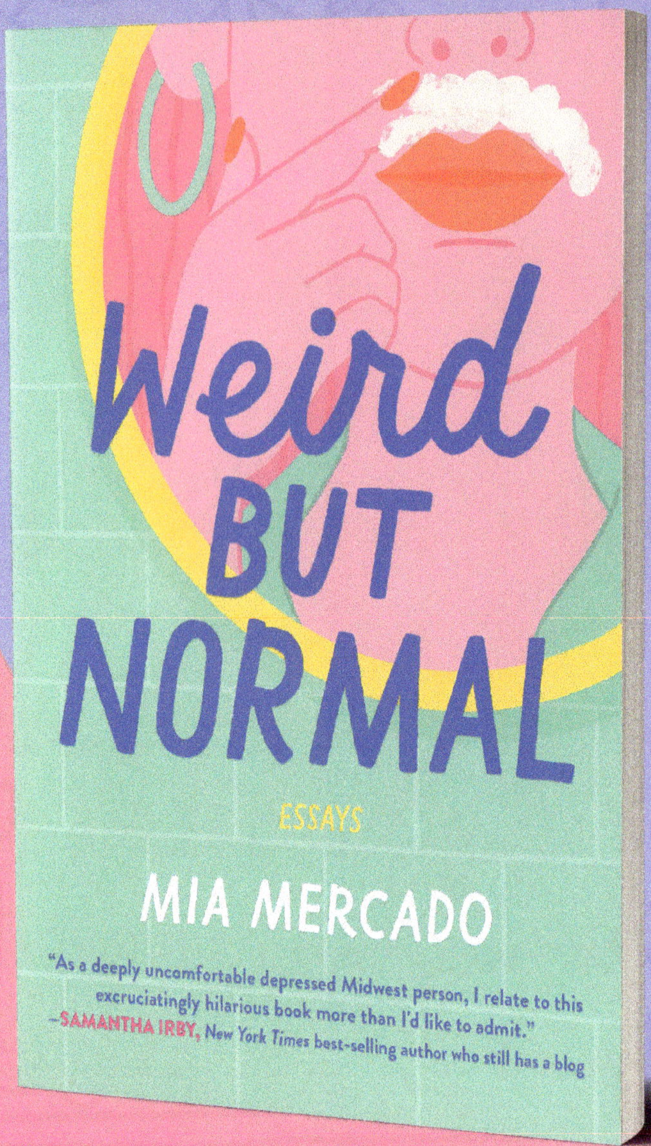
Weird BUT NORMAL
ESSAYS
MIA MERCADO
"As a deeply uncomfortable depressed Midwest person, I relate to this excruciatingly hilarious book more than I'd like to admit."
—SAMANTHA IRBY, New York Times best-selling author who still has a blog

"As a deeply uncomfortable depressed Midwest person, I relate to this excruciatingly hilarious book more than I'd like to admit."

—SAMANTHA IRBY,
New York Times best-selling author

"Hilarious, warm, relatable, confessional, and emotional. Her writing leaps off the page! But not literally. That would be horrible. Imagine writing leaping off the page, soiling your house. Just awful."

– MEGAN AMRAM,
writer/producer of
The Good Place & *The Simpsons*

ESSAYS *on the* AWKWARD, UNCOMFORTABLE, SURPRISINGLY REGULAR PARTS *of* BEING HUMAN

including

My Dog Explains My Weekly Schedule • Depression Isn't a Competition, but, Like, Why Aren't I Winning? • Mustache Lady • White Friend Confessional • Treating Objects Like Women

HarperOne   *An Imprint of* HarperCollins*Publishers*   www.harperone.com

LOVE LETTERS

BY MICHAEL GERBER, BIOLOGICAL SON

Happy Mother's Day!

(Guys, I gotta run this right up front or the guilt will be NUCLEAR)

Today is Mother's Day here in America, and as a result I'd like to apologize to my mom, because I just ate a candy bar for breakfast. I also did not use a plate. And since it was 12:07 pm, I didn't technically *have* breakfast which, though my mother would never use the phrase "the most important meal of the day" because she does not deal in commonplaces, I know she feels is *a* meal, and thus somewhat important.

So: only one paragraph in, and already three strikes against me. Or, more to the point, *her*. Even though I'm 50 and well past the age that any parent or indeed even the police or military can control my behavior, I know my mother would feel that my food choice reflected on her, and so I'm sorry. I'm sorry for doing it, and I'm sorry for writing it, so that you all now know about it, which I'm also sorry for.

*"Drink it, asshole! People are judging **me**!"*

But what I'm really sorriest about is that it's Mother's Day at all. When our society doesn't like a group—when they really work 24/7 to screw you over—they give you a day. Or a month, a month is a real fuck-you. If you're the type of person to ask, "Why isn't there a White History Month?" go pound sand, but before you do, just know that if "White History Month" is ever declared—*run*. Ask women and African-Americans, if you don't believe me.

There is no, for example, Billionaires' Day. I feel like an idiot for even typing that. Every day is Billionaires' Day, we all know that, deep down in our bones and bank accounts. Nothing is more important. For a week or two in March, there seemed to be some chance that Billionaires' Day would be put on hold, just temporarily, but no. The whole society can collapse—or you can die which, to you, would be worse—and America will still celebrate Billionaires' Day. Every day.

I'm not saying we should cancel Mother's Day, especially not this year. My own mom, a smart and forward-thinking woman, has laid in enough other children and grandchildren to distract herself from my affairs; would that I had the same option. But COVID hits moms pretty hard. First of all, moms are old, or at least old-ish (though don't tell yours that, at least not today). The older you are, the more COVID's got it in for you, which suggests that it is Earth's natural attempt to cleanse itself of stories about Woodstock. I'm going to avoid mentioning the Sixties for a while, just to flatten the curve.

Also, a lot of the behaviors people are claiming to engage in while quarantined—and let's be honest, we're bragging—directly defy maternal directives. Comb your hair. Wear pants. Don't eat a candy bar at noon and call it breakfast. I don't care what a freethinker she pretends to be, these are all rules your mother is foursquare behind, and don't tell me otherwise. My mom almost took me to Woodstock (oops) and isn't even on Twitter, but every time I post "Still not wearing pants!" I know she *feels* it. Somehow. It's like a disturbance in the Force. Tweets like that are a microaggression, and trust me, that is not a war you want to start. Though we often forget this, mothers are people, and as such frequently experience a strong desire to choke a mofo. Children are not exempt, as you will find out after a few glasses of wine. But because our society frowns upon child-killing, mothers are forced, almost from the moment of conception, to redirect and minimize their anger.

What I'm saying is: mothers are the Sun Tzu of microaggressions. Don't mess with them. Just say "Thank you" over and over as you back out of the room, bowing. You're apologizing for all the horrible stuff you've done and said, plus a whole bunch of gnarly biological shit you don't even know about. For the sake of everyone's dignity, including yours, don't make her go into it. It was hard enough to *smell*.

Finally, if you've lived far away from your mother, as I have for most of my adult life, you're bound to notice that they like it when you're together. Remember, this person spent years guarding the infant you. Whenever you're out of her sight, some part of her brain is whispering, *"But what if there are lions?"* Zoom does not help. Zoom would just preserve a digital record of the attack, which is even worse. What would "a good mother" do? Never watch it again? Re-watch it annually on your birthday, surrounded by black candles? Or put it up on Facebook immediately, to warn all her friends, most of them mothers, about lions eating children—adults, but they'll always be your child—right here in Santa Monica?

There is no good answer. Like my mother is fond of saying, "As a mom, you can never win."

I wonder why she says that? Anyway, love you Mom, happy Mother's Day.

MICHAEL GERBER'S *mother is more attractive, more interesting, smarter, and wittier than he is. But she didn't have his mother. Her art was featured in* **Bystander #2**.

A WARNIN'

BY JACK HANDEY

COWBOY DANCE FUTURE WORLD

"Spin around once, you might be O.K. Spin around twice, and they set the dogs on you."

It is the year 2248. We live in what some would call a perfect world. There is no disease, or hangovers. There is no fighting, except between women, for entertainment purposes. If you hear about a party, they have to let you in. It's the law. And they can't kick you out, no matter what you do.

But there is a dark side to our world. There is no funny cowboy dancing. It is forbidden by the High Council. No one wearing a cowboy hat or cowboy boots may get up in front of others and do a dance that could be considered "outlandish or unserious." This includes funny spinning, funny stomping or funny sashaying. You don't even have to be wearing the cowboy boots on your feet; moving them by hand is also a crime.

The secret police are always looking for the slightest sign of people doing a funny cowboy dance. If you fall down on a slippery floor, then get back up, then fall down, then get up, again and again, you will probably be beaten with billy clubs. Spin around once, you might be O.K. Spin around twice, and they set the dogs on you.

Even the language has been changed. Officially, the word "yee-haw" no longer exists, nor the phrase "Watch me go!" Those found guilty of habitual funny cowboy dancing are either executed or banished to the Desolate Zone, where they are forced to get jobs and raise families. Some have to undergo state-sponsored "dance therapy." When you come out, they say, the only kind of cowboy dancing you're interested in is cowboy ballet, which nobody likes.

It's no longer safe to wear a cowboy hat at all. Especially a hat that is comically large or small. A friend of mine was arrested for walking down the street with a tiny Mexican sombrero on his head. He was never seen again.

Despite the perils, there are those of us who have vowed to keep funny cowboy dancing alive. We have learned to recognize each other. When I meet someone, I might cross the room with an exaggerated swing to my arms. If he says, "Why are you walking that way?" I know he's not one of us. But if he approaches me with a little prance, holding his hand up like he's whirling a lasso, I know he's O.K.

No single one of us knows the entire funny cowboy dance. It would be too dangerous. One person might know the bowlegged sideways scoot. Another might know the fake off-balance running-in-place. Yet another could be an expert at the agitated-leg-while-the-other-leg-is-straight. Under torture you might be forced to reveal the cowboy peekaboo, but that's it. That's all you'd know.

How did our society, so enlightened when it comes to things like free telescopes if you live near a girls' college, or mandatory drunk leave, come to this? The terror can be traced to Don, the so-called chairman of the High Council. Many years ago he was giving his annual Big Speech at a mass rally. The speech was not going well. It was long and boring. Don sensed this, and suddenly announced, "Hey, everybody, want to see me do a funny dance?" Without waiting for an answer, he launched into a desperate, flailing flurry. It went on and on, more and more pathetic. When it finally ended, with Don panting and sweating, there was nothing but silence. Then one person applauded. Then another. Then a third. But that was it, three people. And they were all his personal assistants. Then someone yelled, "The funny cowboy dance is a lot funnier!"

Don vowed, then and there, to crush funny cowboy dancing. He even sent a killer robot back through time to kill Jack Handey, the founder of the modern funny cowboy dance. But when the robot saw Handey performing the dance, it was so hilarious he could not kill him.

Upon his return, the killer robot was executed. He was placed, standing up, under a huge hydraulic press. It is said that as it squeezed down upon him, he began doing the funny cowboy dance. He continued dancing until he was only two feet tall. Then his lights went out.

One day again, perhaps, a man will be able to get up and do his funny cowboy dance. Or any kind of dance he wants to do (within reason). He'll be able to throw his cowboy hat on the floor, stomp on it with both feet, then put it back on his head and get a goofy look on his face. He'll be able to pretend to strike a match on his buttock, light an imaginary cigarette, then notice with alarm that his rear end is on fire. All while galloping and tiptoeing and high-kicking to his heart's content.

I don't blame Don. Once, he was my friend. But he was corrupted by being such a moron. And to be honest, not everything he's done has been bad. After all, he did wipe out Shakespeare.

JACK HANDEY *is a novelist and essayist perhaps best known for his "Deep Thoughts" on* **Saturday Night Live.** *His latest book,* **Please Stop the Deep Thoughts,** *can be ordered on JackHandey.com.*

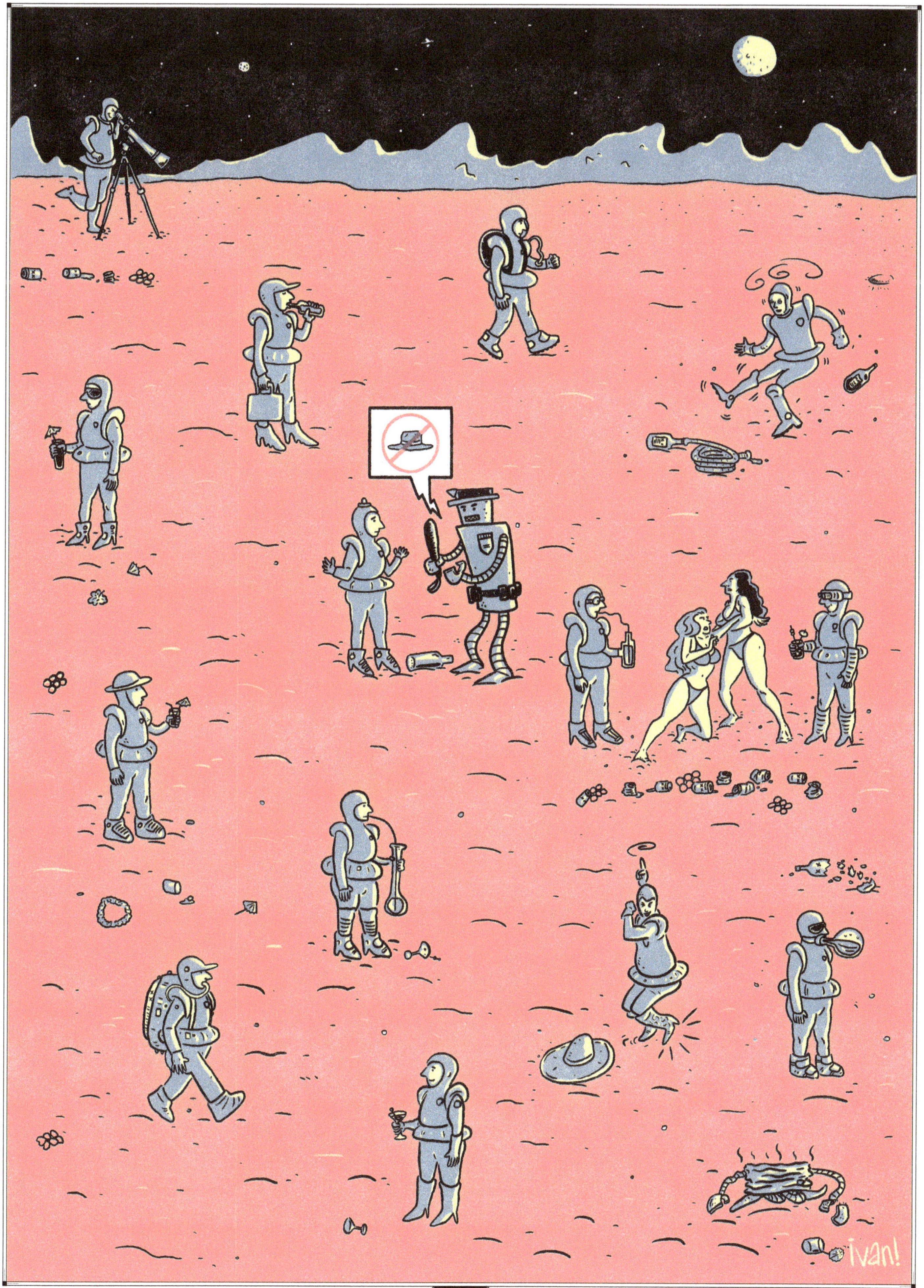
ivan!

DEAD BAROQUE
BY KYLE BERLIN
LIVES OF THE ARTIST
Does the artist live on in their work? And if so, do they pay rent?

ANAXAGORAS
(b. Athens, 460? BCE)

Origins obscure; mentioned in a treatise by Seneca, but no contemporary accounts exist. Pliny the Elder records a contest between Anaxagoras, Zeuxis, and Parrhasius. At his studio, Zeuxis pulled back the curtain from his easel, to reveal a bunch of grapes so lifelike that birds descended from the sky to peck at it. The artists then walked to Parrhasius' studio. In order to reveal Parrhasius' masterpiece, Zeuxis was asked to pull back a curtain, only to find that the curtain itself was the painting. Amazed that such an illusion could deceive a fellow artist, Zeuxis conceded, whereupon the two remaining contestants proceeded to Anaxagoras' studio. Once inside, Anaxagoras asked Parrhasius to close the door, so that his painting might be seen in the proper light. Parrhasius, to his amazement, found that the door that had admitted them was in fact a painting of a door, whereupon Anaxagoras shook his head, turned the handle, and walked into the landscape of his masterpiece, never to be seen again.

CILIEGIOLO
(b. Vincenzo Tornese at Pisa, in Tuscany, 1470/71)

Called 'Ciliegiolo' after a grape varietal indigenous to the region of his birth. Enjoyed advice and support from Augustinian friar and cardinal Giles of Viterbo, as well as frequent commissions from the Duke of Milan. A contemporary of Da Vinci and Michelangelo. Vasari records a contest between the three artists. Da Vinci submitted a portrait of Orpheus so convincing that it produced an audible tone. Michelangelo, in turn, led them to the Sistine Chapel. The artists saw God Himself, reaching out to Adam; there in the gloom, they saw the spark of life to fly between them, as hosts of angels golf-clapped.

The three artists repaired to Ciliegiolo's studio. As befitting Italian custom, Ciliegiolo offered the two great artists wine from his own fields, as they passed their eyes over a modest painting of that vineyard. Da Vinci and Michelangelo, both confident of victory, drank to excess. Upon waking, they were amazed to find Ciliegiolo in the foreground of his own painting, tending to the vines with great care. He waved, then continued trimming in preparation for the following year's harvest. After Ciliegiolo surmounted the nearest hillock, Da Vinci and Michelangelo left, promising never to speak of the sorcery they had witnessed. Not until three years later, after each received a case of the wine at their respective villas, in Florence and in Rome, did they finally concede. It was, as Vasari records, 'a vintage most divine.'

BROUSSARD, JEAN-LOUIS
(b. Bouches-du-Rhône, France, 1851)

Fellow inmate of Van Gogh's in the asylum at Saint-Remy-de-Provence. In 1890, Broussard fell hopelessly in love with Marie-Celeste Trabuc, youngest daughter of an asylum orderly. When her parents refused his proposal, he went mad; a subsequent search turned up no sign of the artist, nor of Mlle. Trabuc, who had also disappeared. Van Gogh, shaken, departed for Auvers-sur-Oise in May of that year, taking with him a painting of Broussard's showing a couple—a young girl, and an older gentleman—beside a quaint farmhouse.

'Is it madness to believe the artist lives on in his work?' begins the last letter Van Gogh wrote to his brother. 'Of course it is, dear Theo, I'm not completely crazy. Anyway, could really use a couple tubes of zinc white when you...HOLY SHIT THEO! THE LITTLE COUPLE! THEY'RE HAVING SE-"

MAGRITTE, RENÉ
(b. Lessines, Belgium, 1898)

Moved to Paris as a young man, absorbing Cubism and Futurism in turn, before rejecting them in favor of an object-based Surrealism. Evinced a lifelong fascination with the threshold—especially doorways (*La Victoire*, *The Amorous Perspective*), windows (*Natural Encounters*, *The Key to the Fields*), and even the frame itself (*The Delights of Landscape*, *Composition on a Seashore*)—which he used to conduct frequent inquiries into the nature of perspective and the uncanny.

In the mid-1960s, suffering from pancreatic cancer and near death, Magritte asked his tailor to deliver a bowler hat, charcoal overcoat, white shirt, high collar, and red tie to his flat in Schaerbeek. Awaiting receipt, he painted a fanciful orchard, with espaliered trees bearing apples and little Magrittes. The painting finished, he dressed, then plucked an apple from the canvas, its leaves still attached to the stem. Passing through the Quartier des Fleurs, he turned onto the Boulevard Lambermont, and continued westward until he reached the sea. Below a light blue sky overlaid with wisps of cloud, he buttoned his coat, then set the apple in front of his upturned mouth, as the sea beat slowly against the low stone wall behind him.

B

KYLE BERLIN *has just finished a novel, fulfilling one of his two constitutional obligations as a resident of Brooklyn. He will never, unfortunately, be able to grow a beard.*

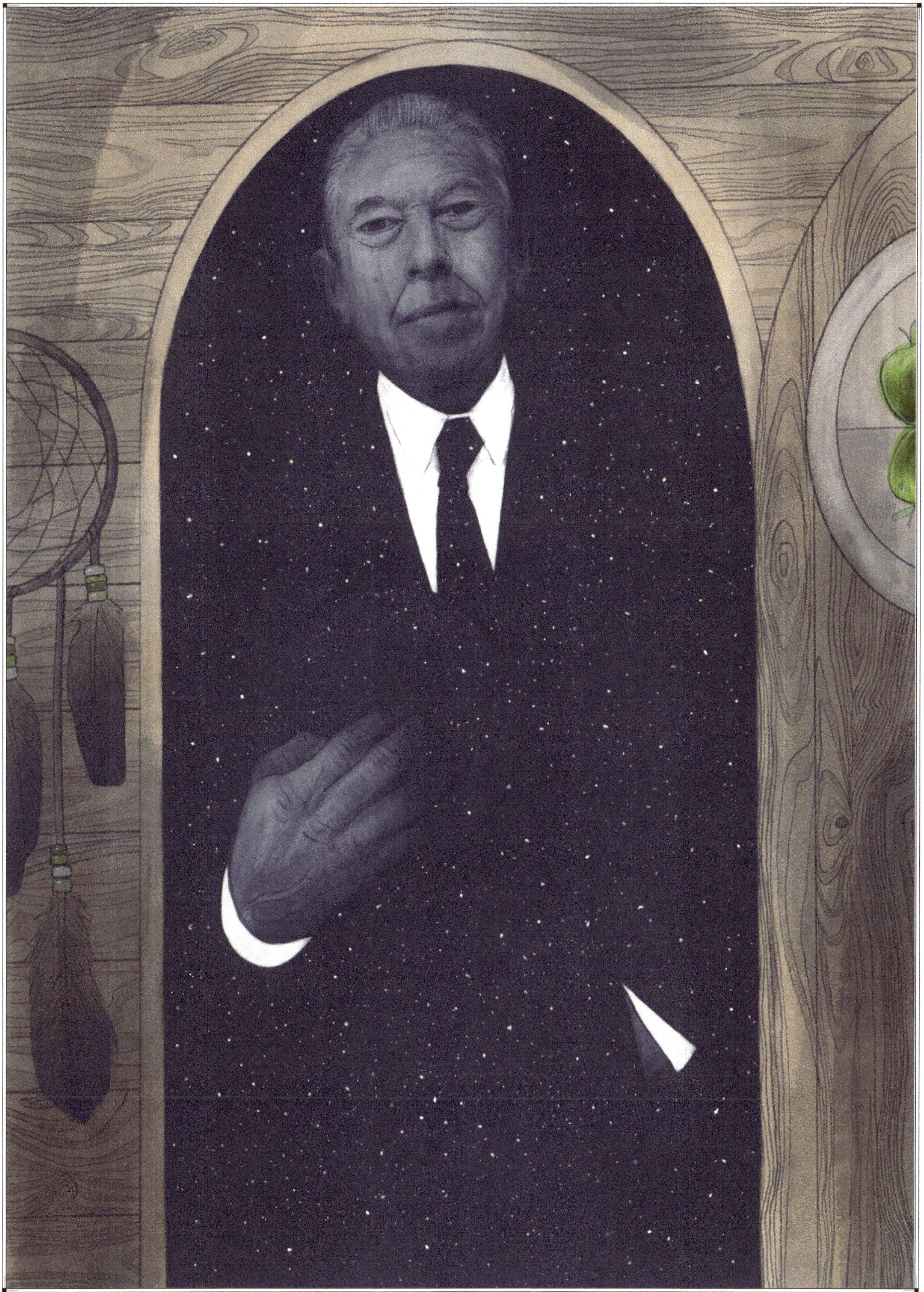

LIFE GOES ON
BY MEG FAVREAU

I'M SORRY THE FIRST MEETING FOR OUR HEIST IS ON ZOOM

Greetings, everyone. I bet you're wondering why I, international playboy/jewel thief Jonathan Bronze, scheduled this videoconference. What I'm about to describe is the most daring, most dangerous—and dare I say, *sexiest*—heist ever attempted.

It's simple: Posing as a pyrotechnic splinter faction of Cirque du Soleil, we're going to infiltrate…oh, shit. Doc Laserman is still in the waiting room. Hold on.

There we go! Everybody wave to Doc.

As I was saying: Boom, flash, *Abbey Road*—and we've liberated the Phoenician Zazzle Emerald from Venice's Millennium Wealth Gala. You're all on mute, so I'll interpret the silence as awe.

I've worked with each of you individually, but we're having this meeting because you need to know each other. Trust each other. *Work as one.* And sure, this isn't the ideal way to meet. We should be in a hypermodern converted loft in Dumbo, a 16th-century French country estate, or—

Hey, Trace Night? It looks like you're trying to say something. No, no, don't unmute. Just put questions in chat. Down on the right-hand side—

Trace, 4:34 pm: *We shud meet in my UDD!!!!*

Much as I love the Underground Darkness Dojo, Trace, all that black velvet would be hell to disinfect. As elite international thieves, we're doing what we do best: adapt. Usually that means improvising a notary's costume, or finding a last-minute security flaw in a cutting-edge vault hiding a priceless cache of long-lost Nazi Picassos. Today, it means firing up the ol' Zoom.

So, introductions—

Ana, 4:35 pm: *Me first? Toddler issues & might have to jump.*

This reminds me: everyone needs childcare the weekend of October 11-13, okay?

Ana, 4:35 pm: *Regular sitter, knows not to ask questions.*

Great. Ana "Platinum Steel" Guitierrez is our muscle. Currently undercover for our team at MI5, the only thing harder than her muscles is her nerve, and the only thing harder than her nerve is her guns, and the only thing harder than her guns is—

Ana, 4:35 pm: *OMFG Jasmine just reached in her diaper and pulled out the poop with her hand fuccccccccc*

Oh no! Bye Ana! Next, Bruno Marsden is our wheelman—Trace, turn off the potato filter.

Trace, 4:36 pm: TACETATO!!!

Goddamn it, Trace, FOCUS UP. For a genius crypto-hacker, you have the attention span of a subway pigeon.

Bruno here learned to drive on an aircraft carrier when his dad was in the Navy, so he's an expert at cars, the sea, and driving cars into the sea. Say hi, Bruno. Bruno? Shit, you froze. Can you hear me?

Bruno, 4:37 pm: *Excited to pull a Chitty Chitty Bang Bang with you all!*

Hoping it won't come to that. Sonya "Deathtrap: The Trap of Death" Chen is…wait, is someone else in the waiting room?

Unknown, 4:38 pm: *TITTIES TITTIES BOOB BOOB BOOB!!!!!*

Who was that kid?

Trace, 4:38 pm: *He isn't on team? u had that tween last job.*

Trace, "that tween" was MacKenzie Dawson, the youngest person ever to earn a PhD in Explosives from MIT. She's getting her wisdom teeth out that weekend. Maybe we should invite this Titties child. If he was able to hack into our Zoom—

D Laserman, MD, 4:39 pm: *"All Things Considered" said Zoom security is shit*

Seriously? *Seriously?!* Why didn't anyone say anything? The whole point of my having a crew is that you have all the skills I don't have, like knowing when free meeting software isn't safe for an elite heist crew!

Trace, 4:39 pm: *Whut r yr skills anyway?*

Everything! Thinking of stuff to steal! Planning! Looking good in a suit! Women-kissing! Occasional gun!

Fine. Shit. Okay, everyone. Stay calm. If more kids come by, we're friends at a happy hour to celebrate Trace's birthday.

Trace, 4:39 pm: *HAPPY BIRFDAY TRACETATO!!!*

TURN OFF THE GODDAMN POTATO OR I WILL STEAL THIS EMERALD JUST TO SHOVE IT UP YOUR ASS!

Sorry, everyone. I know my affable-yet-steely calm is the glue that ties this team together. We still have four months until the Wealth Gala, plenty of time to—

Bruno, 4:40 pm: *you see the gala was pushed to '21? Covid*

GOD FUCKING DAMN IT. Okay, this is very important. Each of you *must*—

Your meeting has ended. If you'd like to schedule longer meetings, please upgrade your account.

MEG FAVREAU (@megfavreau) *lives in Los Angeles, where she writes for animated series and regularly dresses up as a giant eye. You can see more from her at* megfavreau.com.

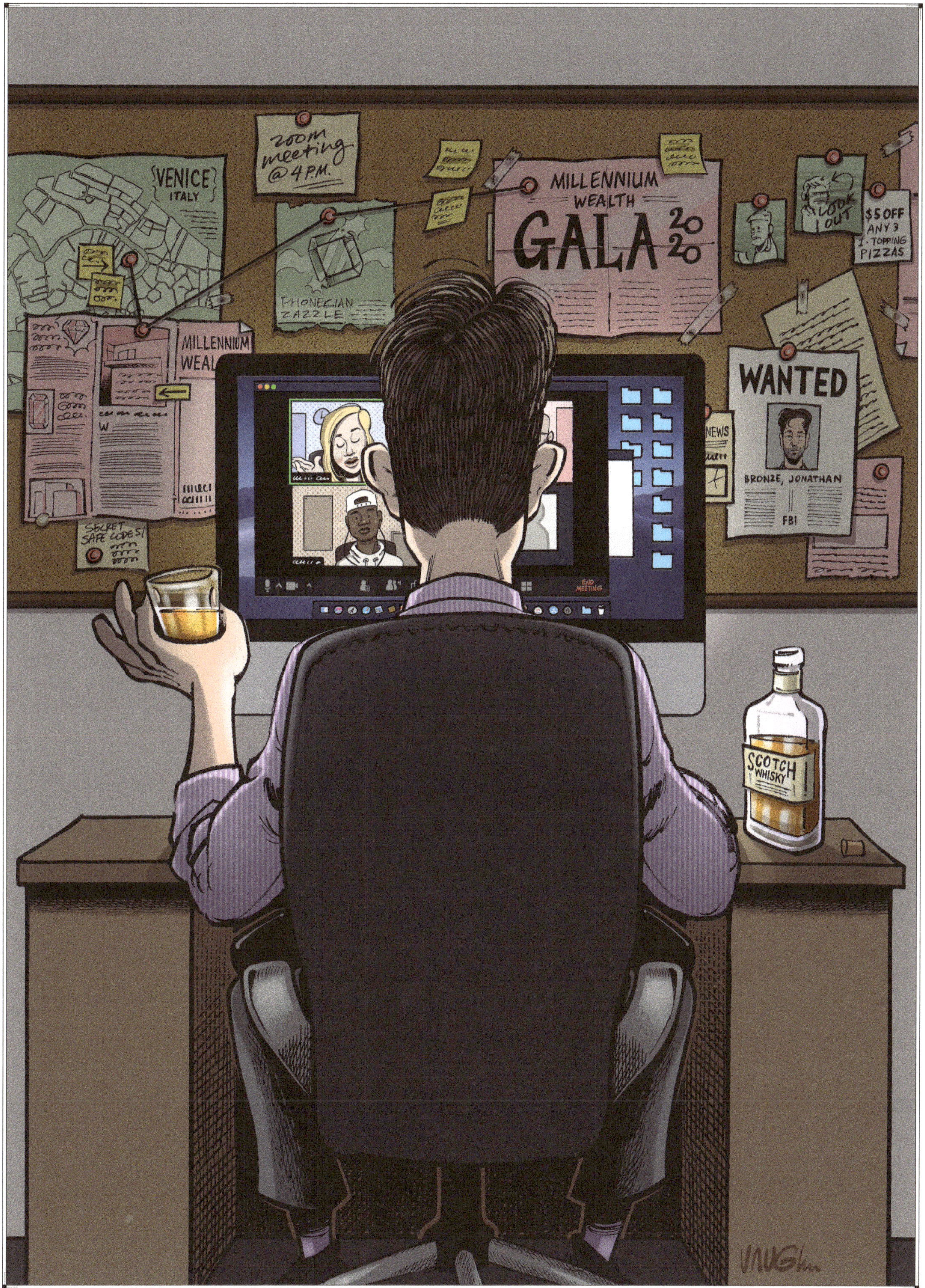
zoom meeting @ 4 P.M.
VENICE ITALY
MILLENNIUM WEALTH GALA 2020
LOOK OUT
$5 OFF ANY 3 1-TOPPING PIZZAS
PHONECIAN ZAZZLE
MILLENNIUM WEAL
SECRET SAFE CODES!
NEWS
WANTED
BRONZE, JONATHAN
FBI
END MEETING
SCOTCH WHISKY
VAUGHN

"OWL SUE!"

BY JOE JANES (& MIKE G.)

DON'T REOPEN HOGWARTS!

Sadly, COVID-19 will not disappear with a wave of the wand

Dear Parents:

My name is Adjunct Professor Tim Smith. For those of you who don't know me, since 2017 I've taught Health here at Hogwarts School of Witchcraft and Wizardry. I am also the volleyball coach.

Before anyone asks, "Tim Smith" is indeed my real name. This being Hogwarts, everyone expects something like "Valerio Flippitysnitz." To be brutally honest, I'd probably get more respect if it were. There's a lot of soft bigotry in the wizarding world, especially when the Tories are in charge.

Being part-time means I have to commute. I went to a holiday feast my first year, to show them I'm a team player. I got sat at a small folding table with a few other adjuncts way in the back. I have never been sorted, by the way. I didn't go to Hogwarts; I went to a mystical community college in Las Vegas run by Penn & Teller. They're wizards. Sorry, I probably shouldn't have told you that. That's okay; they have spells that can selectively obliviate memories on entire populations. Remember when Penn had a ponytail? If you don't, it worked.

But for all this, I love Hogwarts, and consider it to be my home, at least here in the physical plane. That's why I'm sending you this owl. (Please tip it generously.) I am sure you have all heard from Headmaster Dumbledore saying "everything is fine" and the school will follow "all MNHS guidelines."

This is yet more crazy talk from an administrator whose first statement on COVID-19 was a mealy-mouthed half-spell on "coven immunity." You don't have to know Latin to see that Albus Dumbledore is more concerned about his cash flow than your child's well-being.

What do "safety precautions" even mean at Hogwarts? Dementors in every hallway? What if someone gets COVID-19? Are we going to lock down the campus and clean it? Do you know how many secret chambers and passageways there are? We have one custodian with a nasty cat. It would take him ages to scrub down everything, even with magic, which, according to the MNHS, only kills about 55% of the germs. Better off arming Dumbledore's Army with a bunch of disinfectant wipes!

I know many of you think COVID is a "Muggle hoax," but wizards have bodies, too. We can mess around with it, but we're still just skin bags filled with blood, bones, and farts. Even if you change into a cat, you are a human in the form of a cat. And regardless of what you read on social media, butterbeer does not prevent coronavirus. It just gets you drunk on saturated fats.

Dumbledore says, "Henceforth, we shall all wear masks." And that's great advice—for Muggles. But if *I'm* in a closed space filled with witches and wizards? I want to see whose lips are moving, in case they are whispering an incantation to make me vomit snails. Again.

And social distancing? Be real. These are kids. Teenagers. Raging hormones mixed with magic skills topped off with undeveloped brains. Get my drift? You know what they have me teach in the Sex Education part of my class? Abstinence. You know what abstinence gets you? About three "magical" teen pregnancies every academic year. And the STI's—by the time the average Hogwesian enters their Seventh Year, they've had at least one case of Dick Pixies. Magic does not supercede biology; it *amplifies* it.

Look, there are many great things about Hogwarts. They won't let us unionize, but it's still better than doing alchemy for some defense contractor. Let the Muggles reopen their schools; Hogwarts should stay closed. I get it, Hogwarts can't go online because no computers, no electricity. *So use astral projection.* I've been working as an astrally-projected personal trainer/artists' model for years. Dumbledore knows this. He's hired me at least twenty times, but never seems to paint anything.

But our beloved Headmaster will never agree to it, and we all know the reason: Money. The movies are over, so that sweet, sweet licensing gold has slowed to a trickle. Book sales are down, and nobody's buying the merch, either. If students don't come to the school in the fall, Dumbledore's gravy train will remain stuck at Platform 9 ¾.

Parents, the students of Hogwarts and their instructors should not be meeting in person. It's not healthy for anyone. Not until there's an effective philtre. Mediwizards say that's a year away, even with Time Turners.

I'm an adjunct, so they won't listen to me. But maybe they will listen to you. Protect your child and your money; I urge you to send Headmaster Dumbledore a howler immediately.

PLEASE DO NOT REPLY, as I live in a bedsit in Scunthorpe. My Muggle landlady is already asking "what's with all the owls?" I can obliviate her memory, but the guano is another matter, and I have almost certainly lost my security deposit. Thank you. *Exitio!*

JOE JANES (@joejanes1065) *is an adjunct professor in the comedy program at Columbia College Chicago and teaches at The Second City Training Center in Chicago. You can lightly stalk him on the socials.*

MICHAEL GERBER (@mgerber937) *runs this magazine. He wrote three book-length parodies of Harry Potter, so when Joe's piece came in…he felt that old magic.*

A graphic novel by famed artist
Robert Grossman

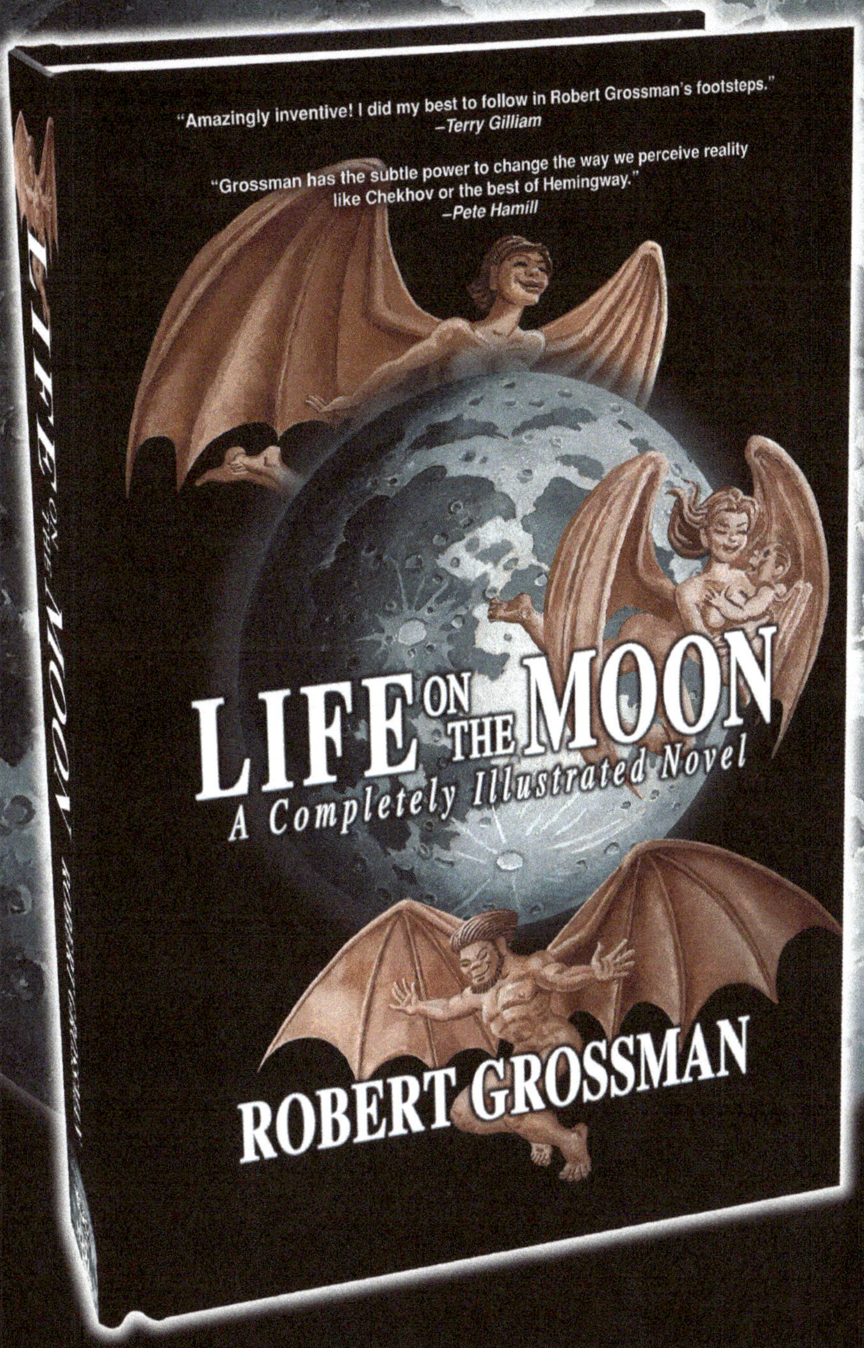

"Amazingly inventive! I did my best to follow in Robert Grossman's footsteps."
—Terry Gilliam

"Grossman has the subtle power to change the way we perceive reality like Chekhov or the best of Hemingway."
—Pete Hamill

LIFE ON THE MOON
A Completely Illustrated Novel
ROBERT GROSSMAN

"History and fantasy join forces!"
—*Rolling Stone*

"Amazingly inventive! I did my best to follow in Robert Grossman's footsteps."
—*Terry Gilliam*

"Like Chekhov or the best of Hemingway."
—*Pete Hamill*

YoeBooks.com

BY BRONZE TEDDY ROOSEVELT

PLEASE TAKE ME DOWN

Also, not urinating in front of me would be bully

Dear President Futter:

I, the statue of Teddy Roosevelt in front of the American Museum of Natural History, do humbly request you take me down.

First, there are the humanitarian reasons. I have been on this horse since 1939. If I had known I would last so long, I would've chosen a slightly less erect posture. My back is killing me. My rear-end is raw. Indubitably.

But my trials, though intense, are nothing compared to those of my colleagues, Fred and Terry. They aren't even wearing shirts; that's three-season discomfort, madam. Terry says "Pants are a human right," and I agree. Then there is the issue of Fred's warbonnet. For the first twenty years or so, Fred didn't complain, he is a trouper. But anything starts to itch eventually.

"Why am I even wearing this thing?" he just asked. "I'm a model from Canarsie."

I have no answer for them. Instead, I have taken up pen and paper, using this horse's head as a writing desk, to write a letter humbly asking for our decommission and removal, preferably indoors or, barring that, to a much warmer climate.

THE MUSEUM CONSIDERS A REPLACEMENT

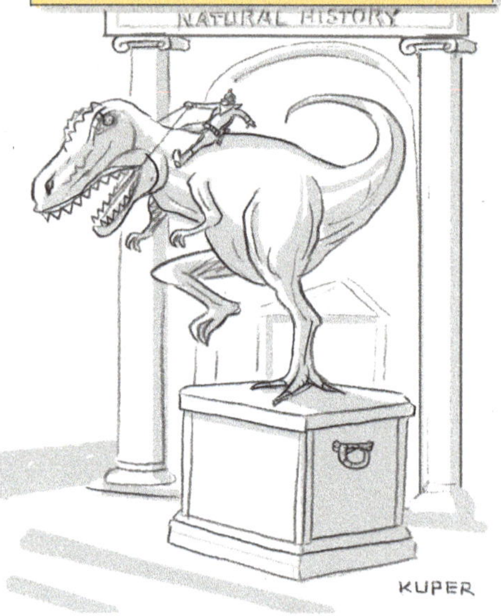
NATURAL HISTORY
KUPER

I have listened to the arguments, such as they are, for extending our service. Primarily they note Mr. Roosevelt's praiseworthy achievements as a trust-buster and protector of the American wilderness.

Well, I can't keep up on the news as much as I'd like, but occasionally a front page does blow across my face, and…I think those two areas in particular are pretty fucked up, don't you?

Excuse my language, but this situation is dire. The three of us believe that any statue requiring 24/7 police protection is probably ready for retirement. (I've heard Boca is nice.)

If the goal of statuary is to encourage certain values—in this case, preventing Satanic corporate accretions from dominating and choking our society; and protecting our precious national lands from despoilage—I think we can all agree that I and my colleagues here are not doing a bang-up job.

(I do not include the horse in this. The horse has nothing to be ashamed of. I can only call him "the horse" because I do not recall his name. C-something, I think it was, or G-something. For the last 60 years or so he has become silent and resentful. I do not blame him. He's standing on metal, must be hell on his knees. But people are treating horses better since 1939, and this is progress. But the other stuff? The Roosevelt stuff? Not so much.)

When the protestors come, I long to say to them, "Yes! I am *with you*. Did you know I was friends with Booker T. Washington? We had dinner together at the White House! I know that doesn't seem like a big deal now, but people were *even more* crazy-racist then."

But I can only sit here, mute, resolute, slightly constipated. I can only imagine how Fred and Terry and G-something feel.

Perhaps it is time for a new statue? Or, dare I say, another approach altogether? If the goal is commemoration, no mere statue can do that; each era selects from the past what it finds praiseworthy, based on what the present requires. Forced commemoration, commemoration that breeds conflict, is worse than useless; it is a marker of what should, indeed must, be ignored, discarded, destroyed.

If the purpose of our eternal suffering is education, here's a radical idea: how about teaching? Are there no schools, no textbooks, no teachers? Surely that little device everyone is staring at as they walk by could inculcate future generations more efficiently than Fred and Terry and G-something. Yes, back in the old days it was different. But if the Romans had invented the internet, I don't think I'd be sitting here getting shat upon, do you?

From what I hear, the four of us are actually preventing people from going into the Museum. Just yesterday I heard one large quasi-child say to the other, "Nah, I've never gone in. Buncha old-tymey bullshit." Yes, he used the "y." Fred and Terry will back me up on this.

What you do with us post-removal is up to you. All we ask is, make it a spot with few urinating drunks or amorous couples—what my colleagues and I have seen in our tyme… it's been a Rough Ride. Indubitably.

Thanks for your attention to this matter. **B**

THE STATUE *of Teddy Roosevelt would like to be moved inside a museum where it's warm and there are no pigeons. He resents your writing on the horse's foot with a gold Sharpie.*

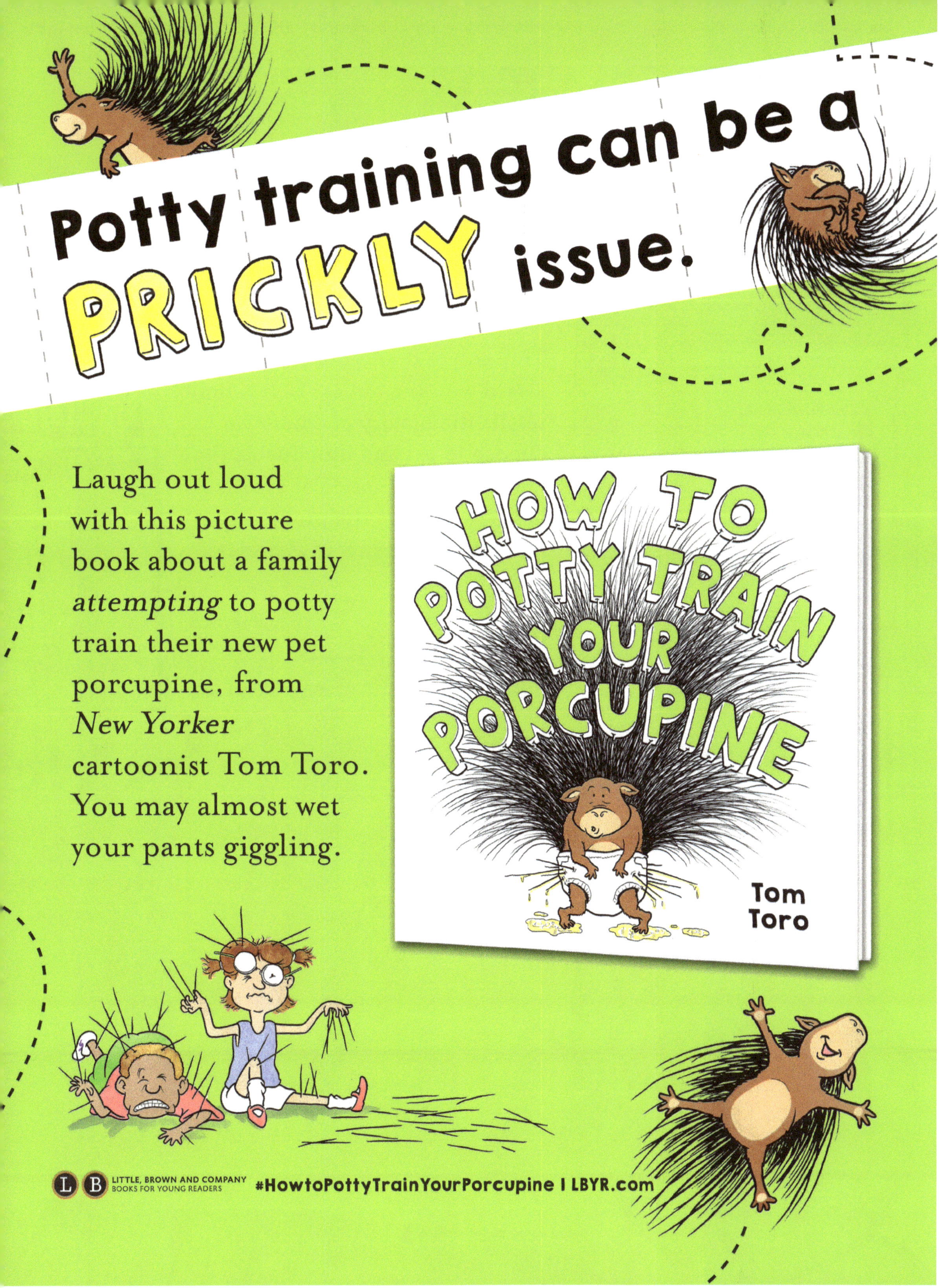
Potty training can be a PRICKLY issue.
Laugh out loud with this picture book about a family *attempting* to potty train their new pet porcupine, from *New Yorker* cartoonist Tom Toro. You may almost wet your pants giggling.
HOW TO POTTY TRAIN YOUR PORCUPINE
Tom Toro
LITTLE, BROWN AND COMPANY BOOKS FOR YOUNG READERS
#HowtoPottyTrainYourPorcupine I LBYR.com

THE DAIRY RESTAURANT

BEN KATCHOR

"KATCHOR SEES INTO THE LIFE OF EVERYTHING HE TOUCHES.... Nothing fails to interest him. I want to sit next to nobody but him on my next international flight."

—ALEXANDER THEROUX, AUTHOR OF *DARCONVILLE'S CAT*

Through text and drawings, award-winning author Ben Katchor retells the history of where we choose to eat and illuminates the historical confluence of events and ideas that led to the proliferation of dairy restaurants in America.

"This **GRAPHIC HISTORY** shows again Katchor's gimlet eye for **CURIOUS CONNECTIONS** and obsessive attention to detail."

—PUBLISHERS WEEKLY

"An informative, **NOSTALGIC** evocation of a **SPECIAL** urban dining experience."

—KIRKUS REVIEWS

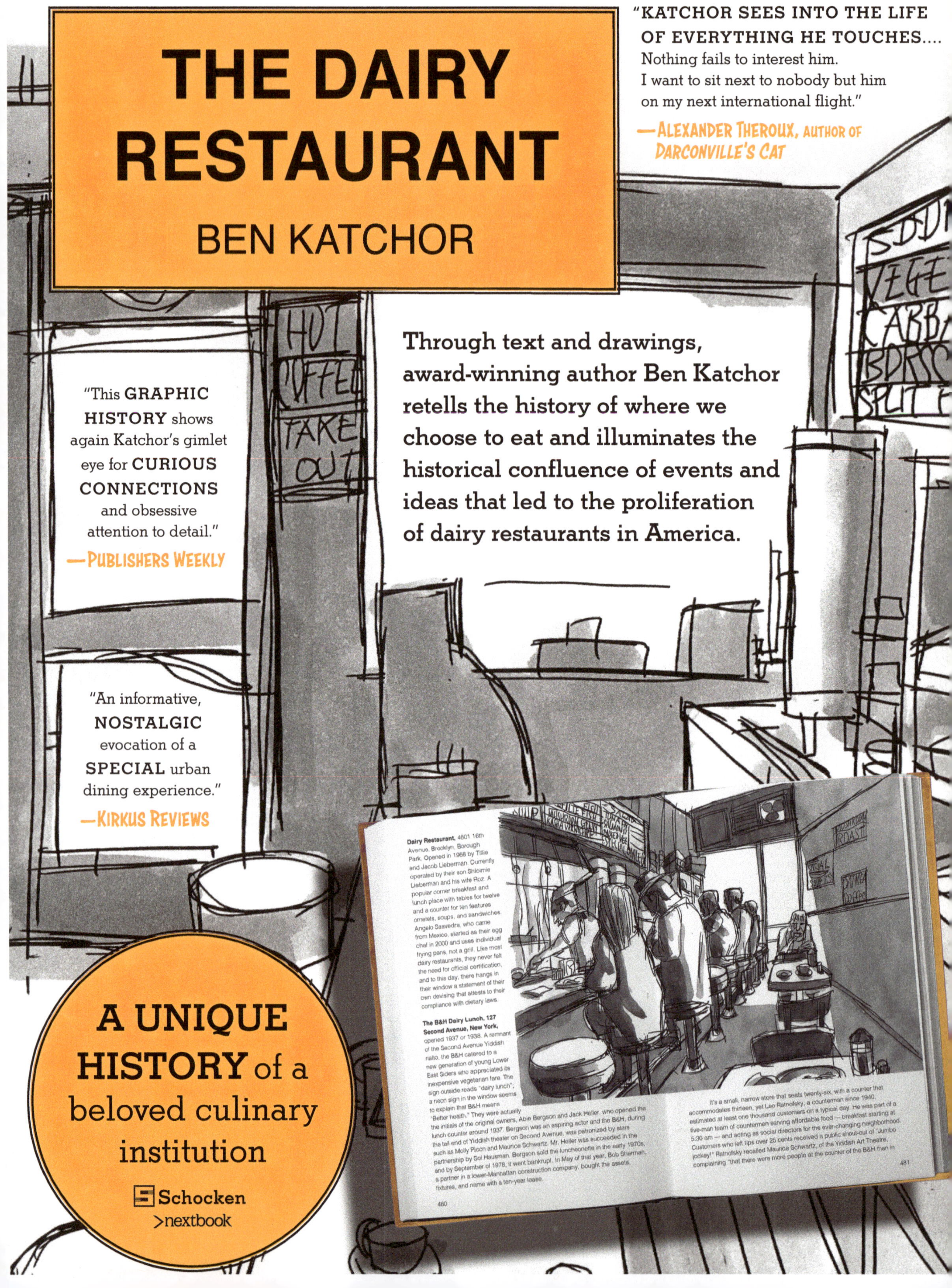

Dairy Restaurant, 4801 16th Avenue, Brooklyn, Borough Park. Opened in 1968 by Tillie and Jacob Lieberman. Currently operated by their son Shloimie Lieberman and his wife Roz. A popular corner breakfast and lunch place with tables for twelve and a counter for ten features omelets, soups, and sandwiches. Angelo Saavedra, who came from Mexico, started as their egg chef in 2000 and uses individual frying pans, not a grill. Like most dairy restaurants, they never felt the need for official certification, and to this day, there hangs in their window a statement of their own devising that attests to their compliance with dietary laws.

The B&H Dairy Lunch, 127 Second Avenue, New York, opened 1937 or 1938. A remnant of the Second Avenue Yiddish rialto, the B&H catered to a new generation of young Lower East Siders who appreciated its inexpensive vegetarian fare. The sign outside reads "dairy lunch"; a neon sign in the window seems to explain that B&H means "Better health." They were actually the initials of the original owners, Abie Bergson and Jack Heller, who opened the lunch counter around 1937. Bergson was an aspiring actor and the B&H, during the tail end of Yiddish theater on Second Avenue, was patronized by stars such as Molly Picon and Maurice Schwartz. Mr. Heller was succeeded in the partnership by Sol Hausman. Bergson sold the luncheonette in the early 1970s, and by September of 1978, it went bankrupt. In May of that year, Bob Sherman, a partner in a lower-Manhattan construction company, bought the assets, fixtures, and name with a ten-year lease.

480

It's a small, narrow store that seats twenty-six, with a counter that accommodates thirteen, yet Leo Ratnofsky, a counterman since 1940, estimated at least one thousand customers on a typical day. He was part of a five-man team of countermen serving affordable food — breakfast starting at 5:30 am — and acting as social directors for the ever-changing neighborhood. Customers who left tips over 25 cents received a public shout-out of "Jumbo jockey!" Ratnofsky recalled Maurice Schwartz, of the Yiddish Art Theatre, complaining "that there were more people at the counter of the B&H than in

481

A UNIQUE HISTORY of a beloved culinary institution

Schocken
>nextbook

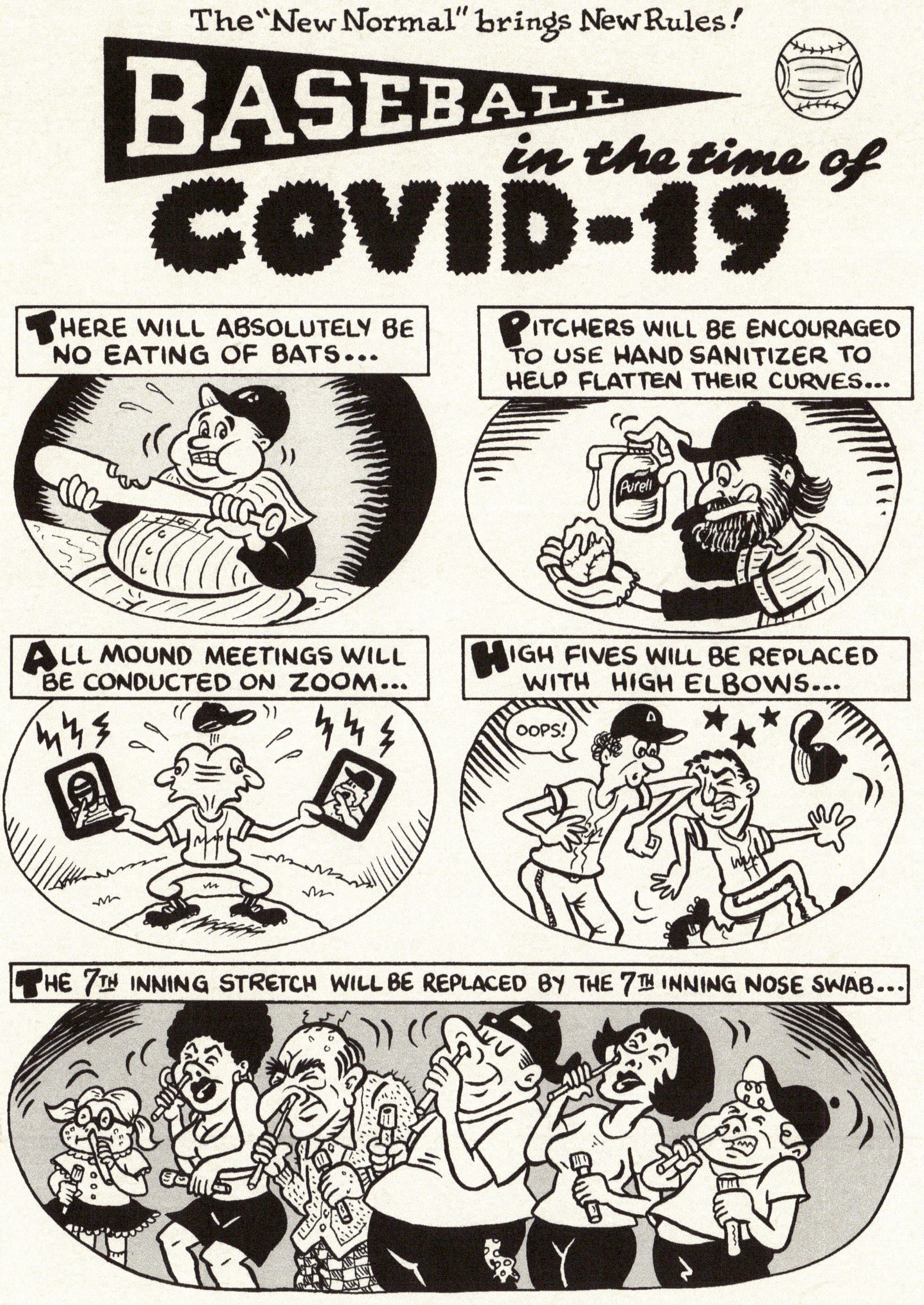
The "New Normal" brings New Rules!
BASEBALL
in the time of
COVID-19
THERE WILL ABSOLUTELY BE NO EATING OF BATS...
PITCHERS WILL BE ENCOURAGED TO USE HAND SANITIZER TO HELP FLATTEN THEIR CURVES...
Purell
ALL MOUND MEETINGS WILL BE CONDUCTED ON ZOOM...
HIGH FIVES WILL BE REPLACED WITH HIGH ELBOWS...
OOPS!
THE 7TH INNING STRETCH WILL BE REPLACED BY THE 7TH INNING NOSE SWAB...

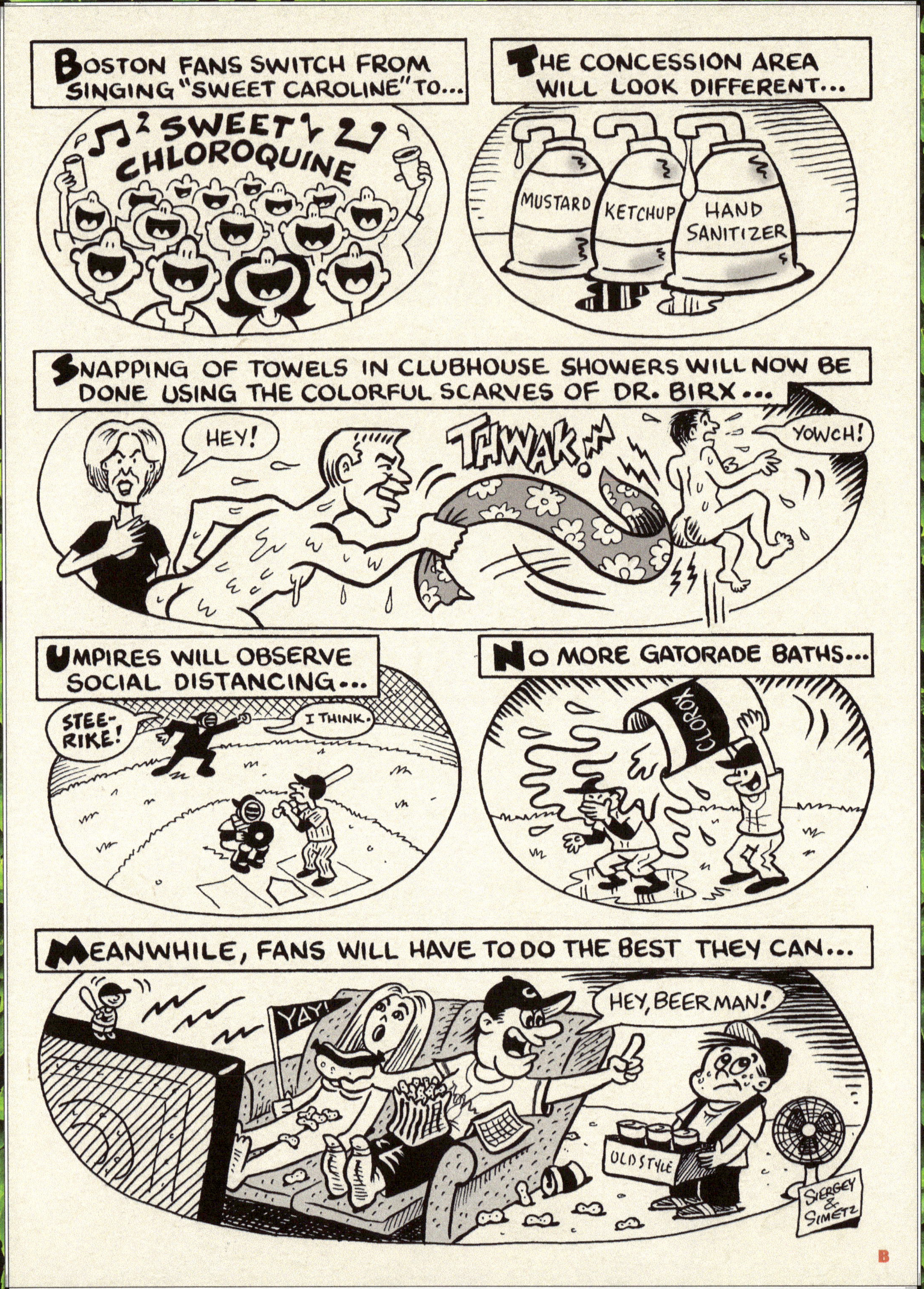

BOSTON FANS SWITCH FROM SINGING "SWEET CAROLINE" TO...
SWEET CHLOROQUINE
THE CONCESSION AREA WILL LOOK DIFFERENT...
MUSTARD
KETCHUP
HAND SANITIZER
SNAPPING OF TOWELS IN CLUBHOUSE SHOWERS WILL NOW BE DONE USING THE COLORFUL SCARVES OF DR. BIRX...
HEY!
THWAK!
YOWCH!
UMPIRES WILL OBSERVE SOCIAL DISTANCING...
STEE-RIKE!
I THINK.
NO MORE GATORADE BATHS...
CLOROX
MEANWHILE, FANS WILL HAVE TO DO THE BEST THEY CAN...
YAY!
HEY, BEER MAN!
OLD STYLE
SIERGEY & SIMETZ

CELADON
BOOKS

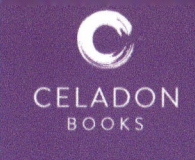

"BOYLAN'S WRY WIT, WICKED SENSE OF HUMOR, AND UNIQUE WAY OF TURNING PHRASES SHINE THROUGH…"

~KIRKUS REVIEWS

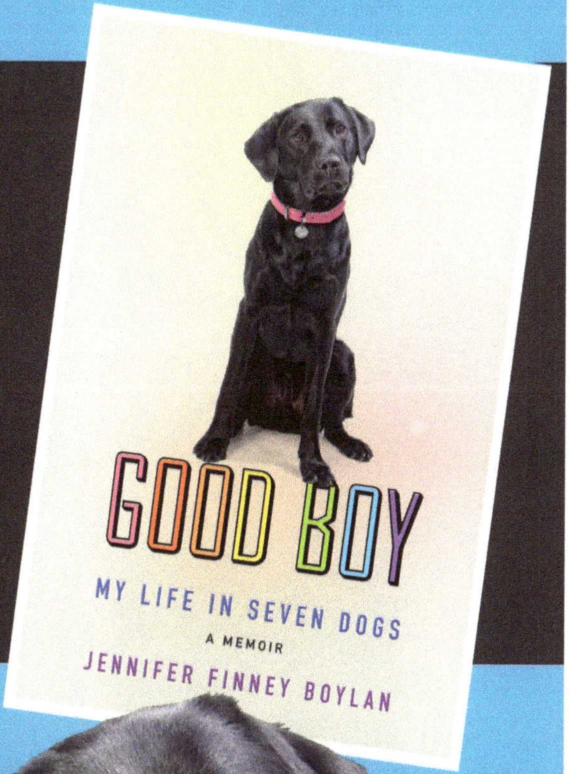
GOOD BOY
MY LIFE IN SEVEN DOGS
A MEMOIR
JENNIFER FINNEY BOYLAN

GOOD BOY

MY LIFE IN SEVEN DOGS

A NEW MEMOIR BY JENNIFER FINNEY BOYLAN, *NEW YORK TIMES* BESTSELLING AUTHOR OF *SHE'S NOT THERE: A LIFE IN TWO GENDERS*

"*Good Boy* is a warm, funny, instantly engaging testament to the power of love—canine and human—to ease us through life's radical transitions. And I say that as a cat person!"

~JENNIFER EGAN
Winner of the Pulitzer Prize and author of *A Visit from the Goon Squad* and *Manhattan Beach*

"Dogs help us understand ourselves: who we are, who we've been. They teach us what it means to love, and to be loved. They bear witness to our joys and sorrows; they lick the tears from our faces. And when our backs are turned, they steal a whole roasted chicken off the supper table."

~JENNIFER FINNEY BOYLAN

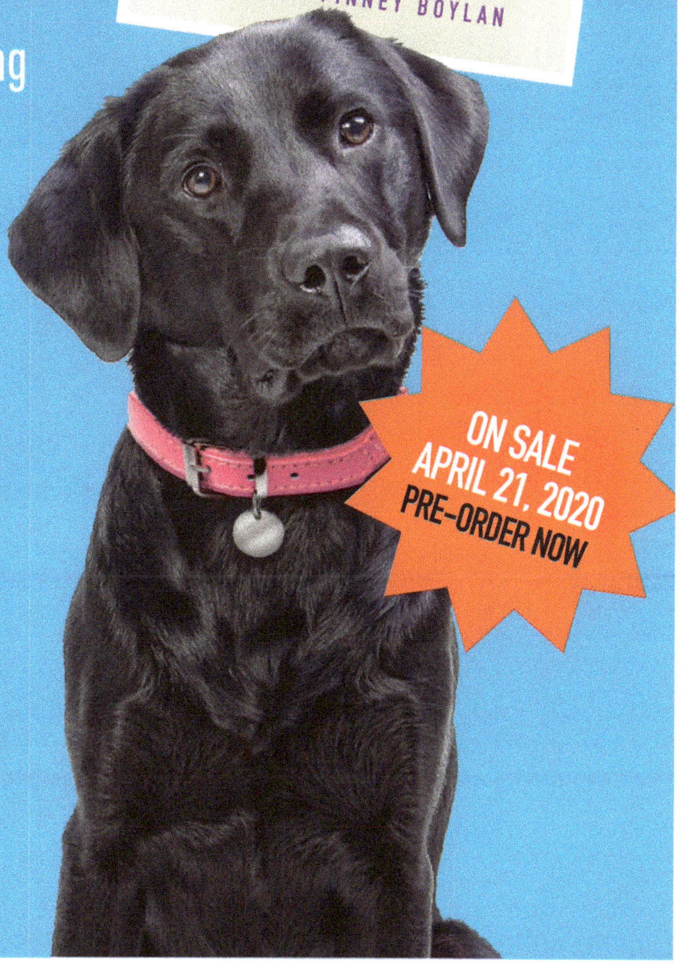
ON SALE
APRIL 21, 2020
PRE-ORDER NOW

CELADONBOOKS.COM/BOOKSHOP

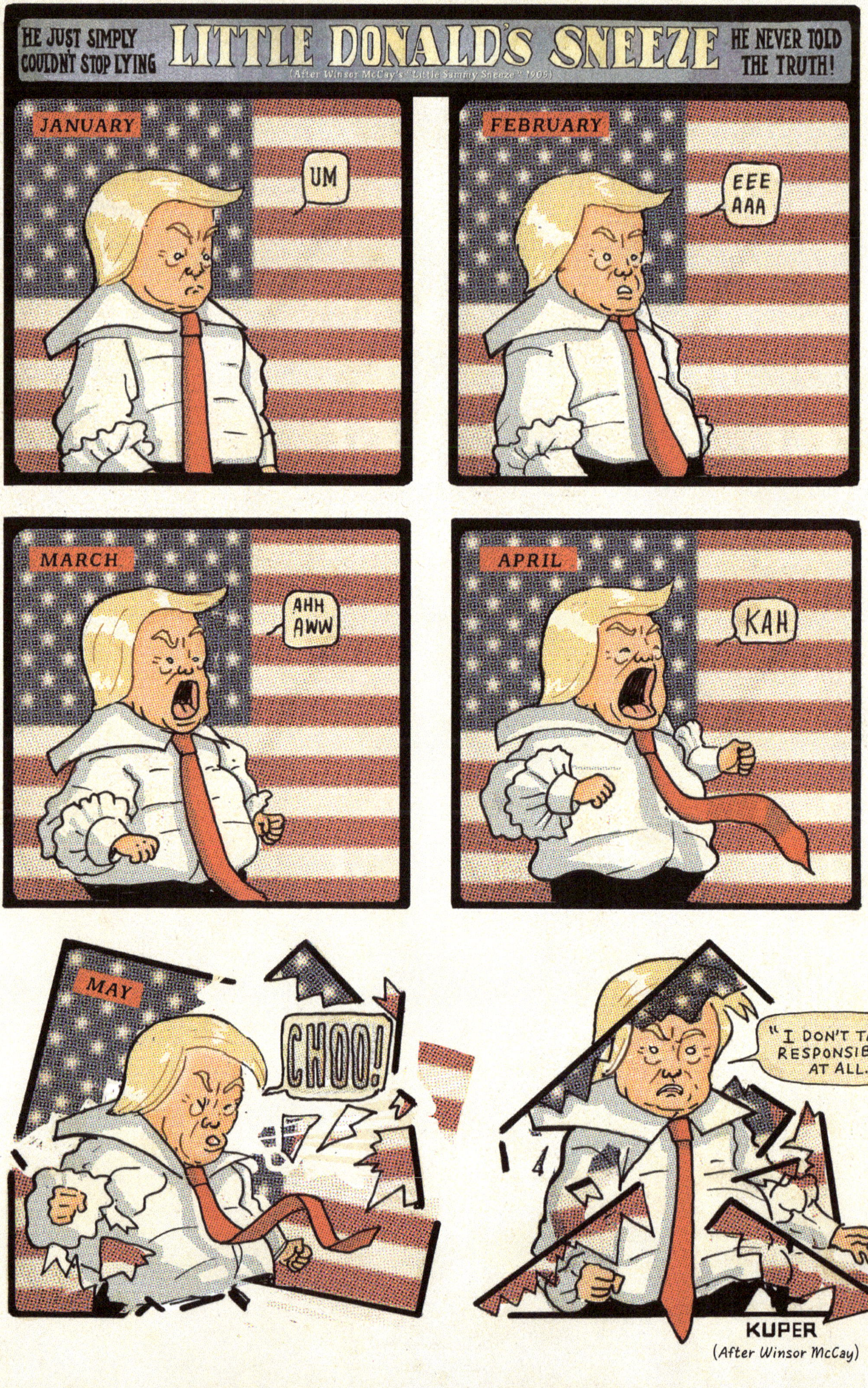
HE JUST SIMPLY COULDN'T STOP LYING
LITTLE DONALD'S SNEEZE
(After Winsor McCay's "Little Sammy Sneeze" 1905)
HE NEVER TOLD THE TRUTH!
JANUARY
UM
FEBRUARY
EEE AAA
MARCH
AHH AWW
APRIL
KAH
MAY
CHOO!
"I DON'T TAKE RESPONSIBILITY AT ALL."
KUPER
(After Winsor McCay)

B.A. Van Sise
My editors have me shooting the news.
I'm literally hanging around hospitals,
doing sad stories every day.
It's awful.

Michael Gerber
Let's get you into #15.
What about that idea we had—
Screenshot portraits via Zoom?

B.A. Van Sise
Better idea:
I'll visit some of your writers/artists.
Photograph them through their windows.
Each one can do what they want with it,
make it their own.

Michael Gerber
Do it!!

WINDOW PORTRAITS
Bystanders Behind Glass

(photos start on the next page)

BARRY BLITT

Western Connecticut.
May 12, 2020

"Seeing this photo makes me realize I really need to work on my core."

R.O. BLECHMAN

*Dutchess County, New York.
May 12, 2020*

"That lock should have a smile. I'm unlocked and doing fine."

ED SUBITZKY

Manhattan, New York.
May 4, 2020

"I was looking forward to seeing this picture.
Or maybe I should say I was looking backward to seeing it.
Now that I've seen it, I can look back to seeing it
and forward to looking back and seeing it again,
and looking back on that, but both backwards
and forwards and back again."

EMILY FLAKE

Brooklyn, New York.
May 3, 2020

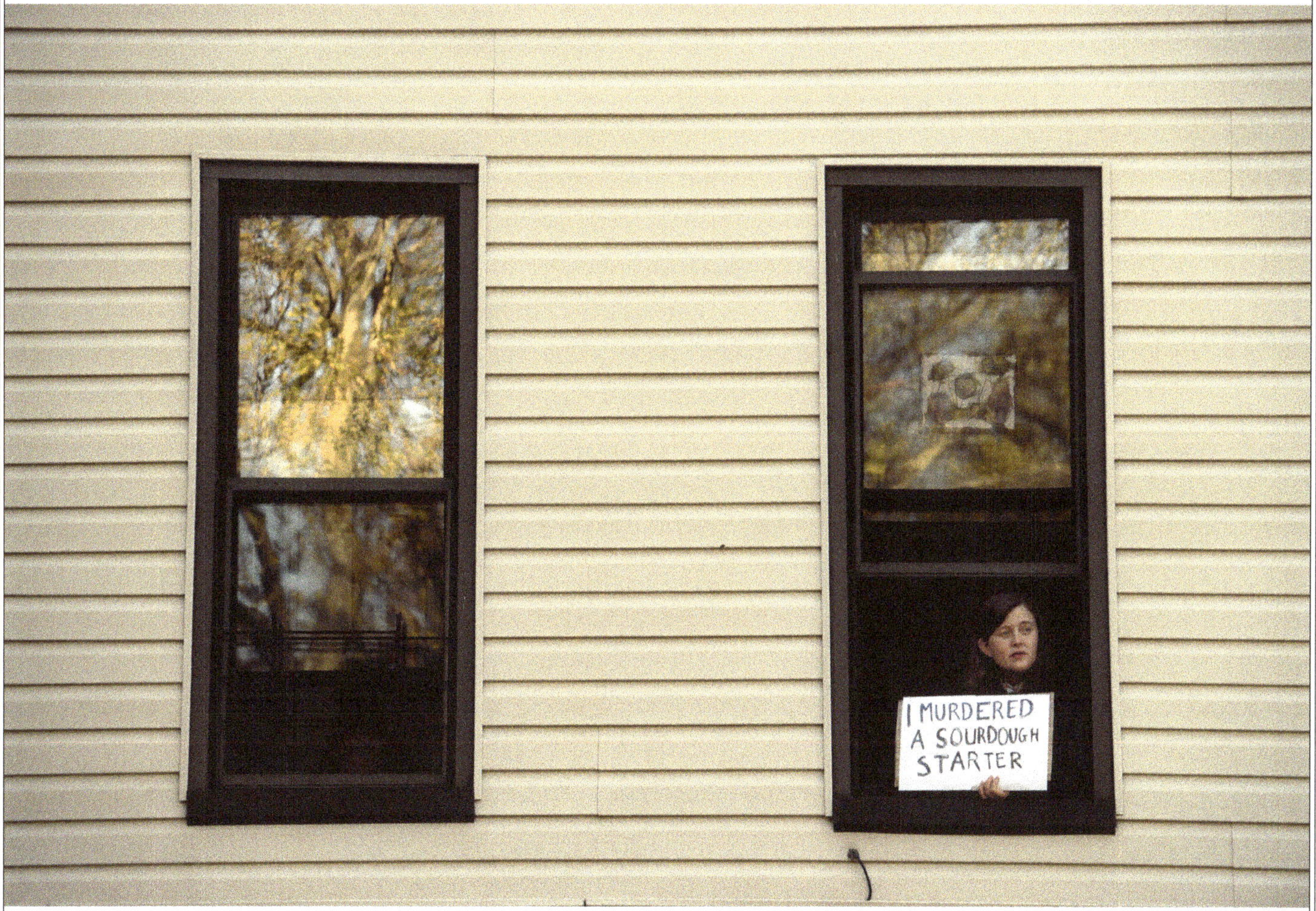
I MURDERED
A SOURDOUGH
STARTER

"...and I'd do it again, too."

M. SWEENEY LAWLESS

*Manhattan, New York.
May 17, 2020*

"Fine. You?"

TRACEY BERGLUND

*Manhattan, New York.
May 14, 2020*

"Yes, I always wear a hat inside my apartment."

ZOE MATTHIESSEN

*New Haven, Connecticut.
May 9, 2020*

"Who needs a salon?"

ED SUBITZKY

Fred's Day

If you want Fred to have a happy day, read only the lines in blue.
If you want Fred to have an unhappy day, read only the lines in red.

Fred Atkinson woke up to the sound of his alarm and thought, "I have a feeling today is going to be just great."
Fred Atkinson woke up to the sound of his alarm and thought, "I have a feeling today is going to be awful."
Fred washed and shaved with a big smile on his face. "Yep," he thought, "this is going to be a good one!"
Fred cut himself while shaving. It was painful and the bleeding wouldn't stop. "Yep," he thought, "it's just starting."
Fred sat down to a tasty breakfast. "Maybe someday," he thought, "I'll find a special someone to share this with."
Gulping down his breakfast, Fred started coughing uncontrollably. "It's those damn allergies again," he gasped.
Traffic was light on the highway, and Fred got to work a bit early. "That'll please the boss," he thought.
As soon as he got on the highway, Fred's car broke down. It took hours for help to come. "I'll be fired," he moaned.
When he got to his desk, Fred was introduced to a new co-worker, Melanie. He thought, "I think I just met my wife."
"When he got to his desk, Fred was introduced to a new co-worker, Melanie. He spilled hot coffee on her dress.
Fred's boss called him in and said, "My boy, we're giving you a big promotion and a substantial raise in salary."
Fred's boss called him in and said, "We're downsizing. Clean out your desk and get out of here now!"
Fred couldn't stop himself from asking Melanie for a date. She said yes, and he left the office floating on air.
Lonely and now jobless, Fred didn't notice a crack in the sidewalk. He tripped and his scalp was gushing blood.
Checking his mail, Fred noticed a certified letter. He opened it up and discovered he had won $10,000 in a raffle.
Fred winced in pain as the ER doctor bandaged his scalp. The doctor looked at him grimly and said, "Hmmmmm."
Fred sat down in his comfortable recliner and sipped some wine while he watched his favorite TV show.
Fred lay uncomfortably in the MRI machine. The doctor said, "I'm afraid you've got a rare and incurable disease."
Checking the rest of his mail, Fred found a report from his doctor that he was in perfect health.
Fred tried to lose himself in his favorite TV show, but right at that moment the cable went out.
Fred couldn't resist calling Melanie. They talked and laughed, as if they had known each other forever.
In despair, Fred called a girl he once had a crush on. She didn't remember who he was.
Fred took a pleasantly, warm shower. He put on his pajamas, all fresh and clean from the laundry.
Something was wrong with the shower. First it scalded him and then no water came out at all.
Fred decided to celebrate a wonderful day with a nightcap. He was feeling all mellow and fine.
Fred felt a stabbing pain in his gut, just as the doctor told him to expect. It spread to every part of his body.
Fred lifted his glass and raised a toast. "To all good things" he said, letting the sweet brandy wash down his throat.
Fred screamed in agony as the pain seared him from inside out, up and down. He wished he had never been born.
"I'm so glad to be alive!" Fred murmured to himself. "And soon Melanie will share all this with me."
"I need some human contact," Fred moaned to the empty air. "I'm all alone, but maybe the radio will work."
Fred decided to end his day with the nightly news. He had a feeling that this time the news would be good.
Fred fumbled for the radio and heard the static-filled voice of a newscaster who sounded very worried.
Fred nodded happily as the newscaster came on and said, "I have something wonderful to tell you folks."
Fred moaned as the newscaster spoke nervously, "I'm afraid I have some very bad news tonight."
"At the UN, all nations agreed to destroy their weapons and enter an age of peace and love."
"At the UN, furious nations have pushed themselves right to the very brink of a world war."
"No more guns, no more missiles, no more hatred, just peace and prosperity for every human being."
"This just in. Radar has shown nuclear missiles heading directly towards us. We are responding in kind."
Fred grinned as the newscaster said, "Sleep well, folks. This has been the day we've all been praying to see."
Fred grimaced as the newscaster said, "Scientists say the chain reaction will destroy the entire universe."

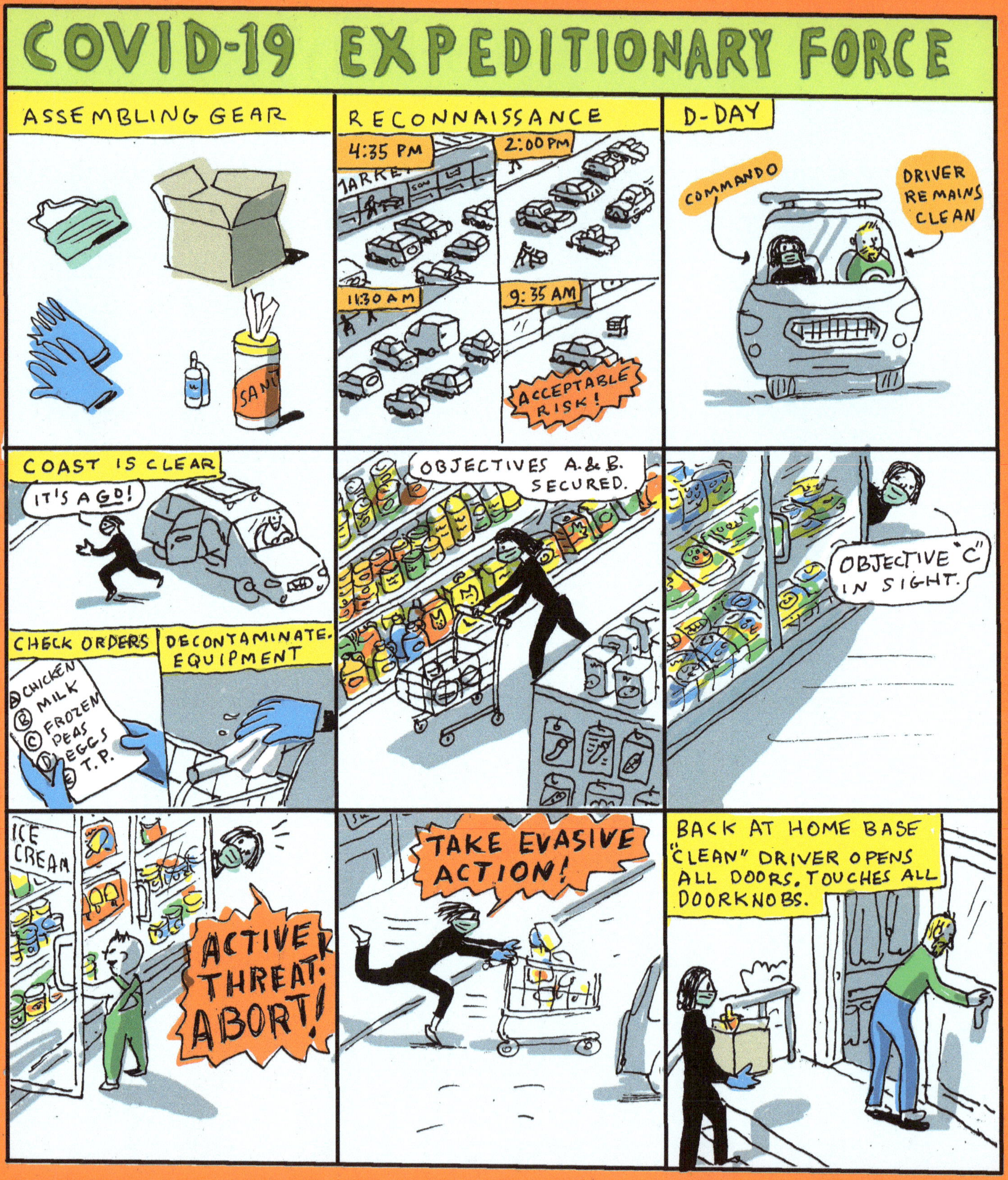
COVID-19 EXPEDITIONARY FORCE
ASSEMBLING GEAR
SANI
RECONNAISSANCE
4:35 PM
2:00 PM
11:30 AM
9:35 AM
ACCEPTABLE RISK!
D-DAY
COMMANDO
DRIVER REMAINS CLEAN
COAST IS CLEAR
IT'S A GO!
CHECK ORDERS
A CHICKEN
B MILK
C FROZEN PEAS
D EGGS
E T.P.
DECONTAMINATE EQUIPMENT
OBJECTIVES A.& B. SECURED.
OBJECTIVE "C" IN SIGHT.
ICE CREAM
ACTIVE THREAT! ABORT!
TAKE EVASIVE ACTION!
BACK AT HOME BASE "CLEAN" DRIVER OPENS ALL DOORS, TOUCHES ALL DOORKNOBS.

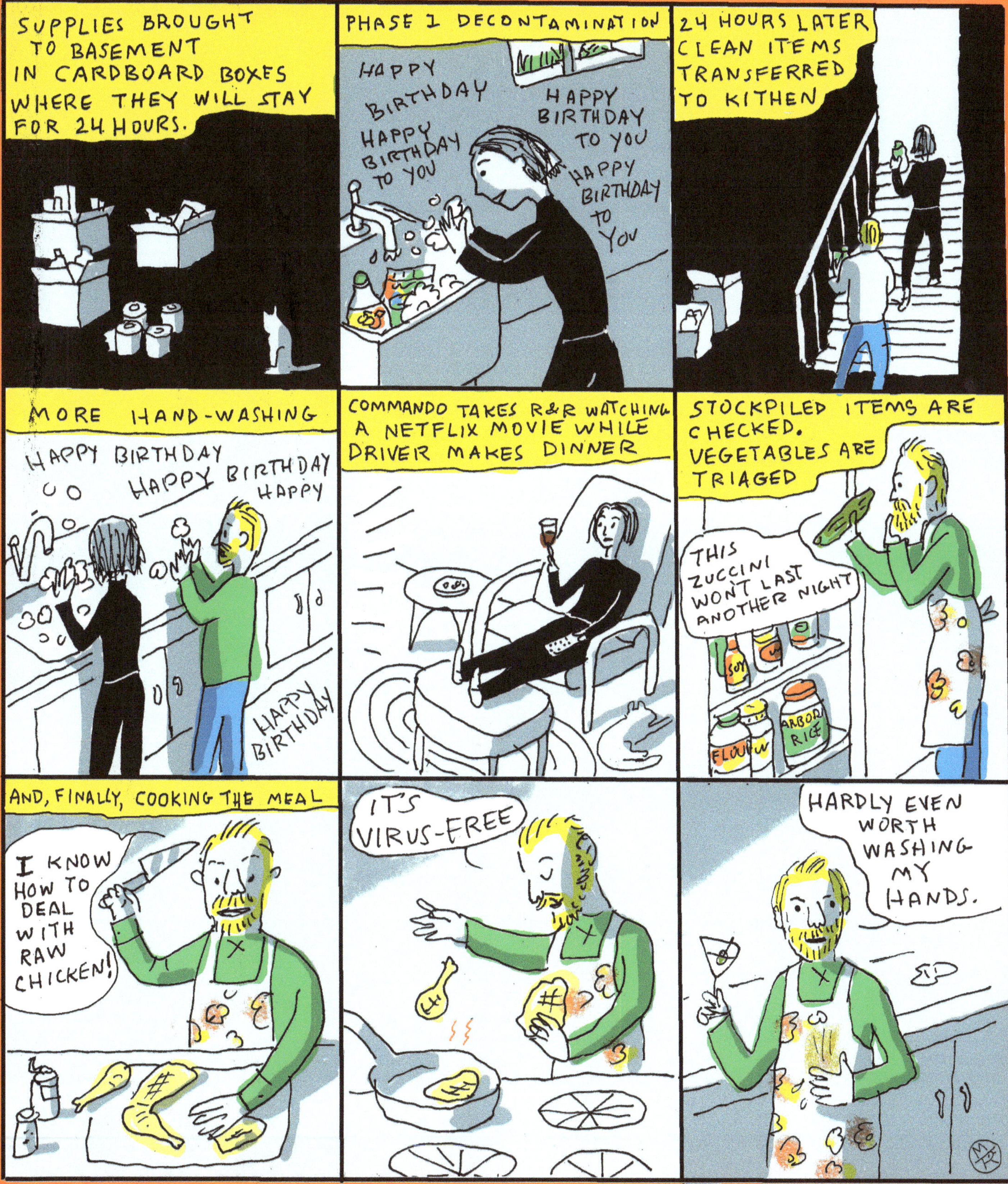
SUPPLIES BROUGHT TO BASEMENT IN CARDBOARD BOXES WHERE THEY WILL STAY FOR 24 HOURS.
PHASE 1 DECONTAMINATION
HAPPY BIRTHDAY
HAPPY BIRTHDAY TO YOU
HAPPY BIRTHDAY TO YOU
HAPPY BIRTHDAY TO YOU
24 HOURS LATER CLEAN ITEMS TRANSFERRED TO KITHEN
MORE HAND-WASHING
HAPPY BIRTHDAY
HAPPY BIRTHDAY
HAPPY
HAPPY BIRTHDAY
COMMANDO TAKES R&R WATCHING A NETFLIX MOVIE WHILE DRIVER MAKES DINNER
STOCKPILED ITEMS ARE CHECKED. VEGETABLES ARE TRIAGED
THIS ZUCCINI WON'T LAST ANOTHER NIGHT
SOY
FLOUR
ARBORIO RICE
AND, FINALLY, COOKING THE MEAL
I KNOW HOW TO DEAL WITH RAW CHICKEN!
IT'S VIRUS-FREE
HARDLY EVEN WORTH WASHING MY HANDS.

Marc Rosenthal *makes illustrations for magazines, both famous and obscure. He is also an author/illustrator of books for children. He lives in the Berkshires in Massachusetts.*

The Assassin

The security checkpoint was dead ahead, and if things today were going to go down, then they would go down right here, right now. They were checking backpacks and purses with flashlights, to make sure you didn't have any bombs. Then, after this, they ran the backpacks, and then the guests, through a metal detector. Just to be on the safe side. Thick Florida sunshine beat down on Molly's face, even at this early hour of the day. From speakers hidden in the flowers came the endless melody. When you wish upon a star, your dreams come true! Yeah, Molly thought. That hasn't exactly been my experience.

"These three remain," her mother had said, when she first came out. "Faith, hope, and love. But the greatest of these is love."

"But mom," she said. "Won't it be a scandal when everyone finds out your son has become your daughter? Won't that be an embarrassment?" The tears had rolled down her face and hung at the bottom of her chin, like raindrops on a downspout.

"Yes," mom said. "But I will adjust."

The security officer—did they call them cast members?—nodded at her respectfully. "Good morning, ma'am," he said. On his lapel was a nametag: STANDHOPE. Molly put her purse down on the table, and the officer shone his pen light into its depths. Then he nodded and handed it back to her. He looked at her dress blues with a phrase pregnant upon his lips. Go on, she thought. Say it.

"Thank you for your service," said Officer Standhope, and she nodded somberly, as if to make clear the depths of the horrors she had witnessed but would not now discuss. The woman on the far side of the metal detector waved her forward, and Molly moved through the portal awkwardly, limping slightly on the fake leg. A piercing alarm went off, and the woman held up her hands, "I'm going to have you stop right there ma'am," she said. Within that single instant three other security guards were on the scene, like they'd all instantly teleported here from the Enterprise.

"It's her leg," said the woman at the x-ray. Her nametag said she was HERNANDEZ.

"I'm wearing a prosthesis," she said, and wondered if she should mention the cancer. She pulled up the cuff of her uniform trousers, revealing the high-tech joint that connected the force sensor in the calf to her dynamic foot. "There's a micro-processor in the knee?"

"Yeah, said Ms. Hernandez. She couldn't be twenty years old. Security at the Magic Kingdom was not exactly the TSA. "Can we run you through again?" Officer Standhope came over and looked at the screen, which the young woman pointed at with a pencil. "I'm looking at that," she said to him quietly.

"Would you like me to go through again, miss?" she said, and turned back, with just the most barely detectable sense of—what would you call it?—nobility striving against humiliation.

"That's okay Lieutenant," said Officer Standhope, with a wave of his hand. "You can go on ahead."

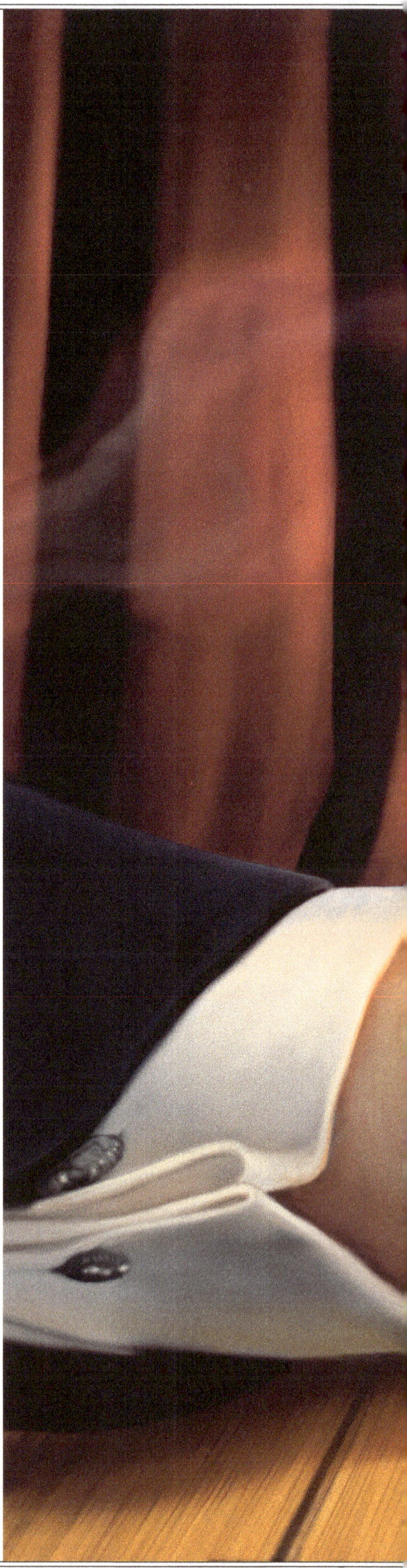

Jennifer Finney Boylan *is* Anna Quindlen Writer-in-Residence at Barnard College. Author of 16 books, she's a contributing opinion writer for *The New York Times.*

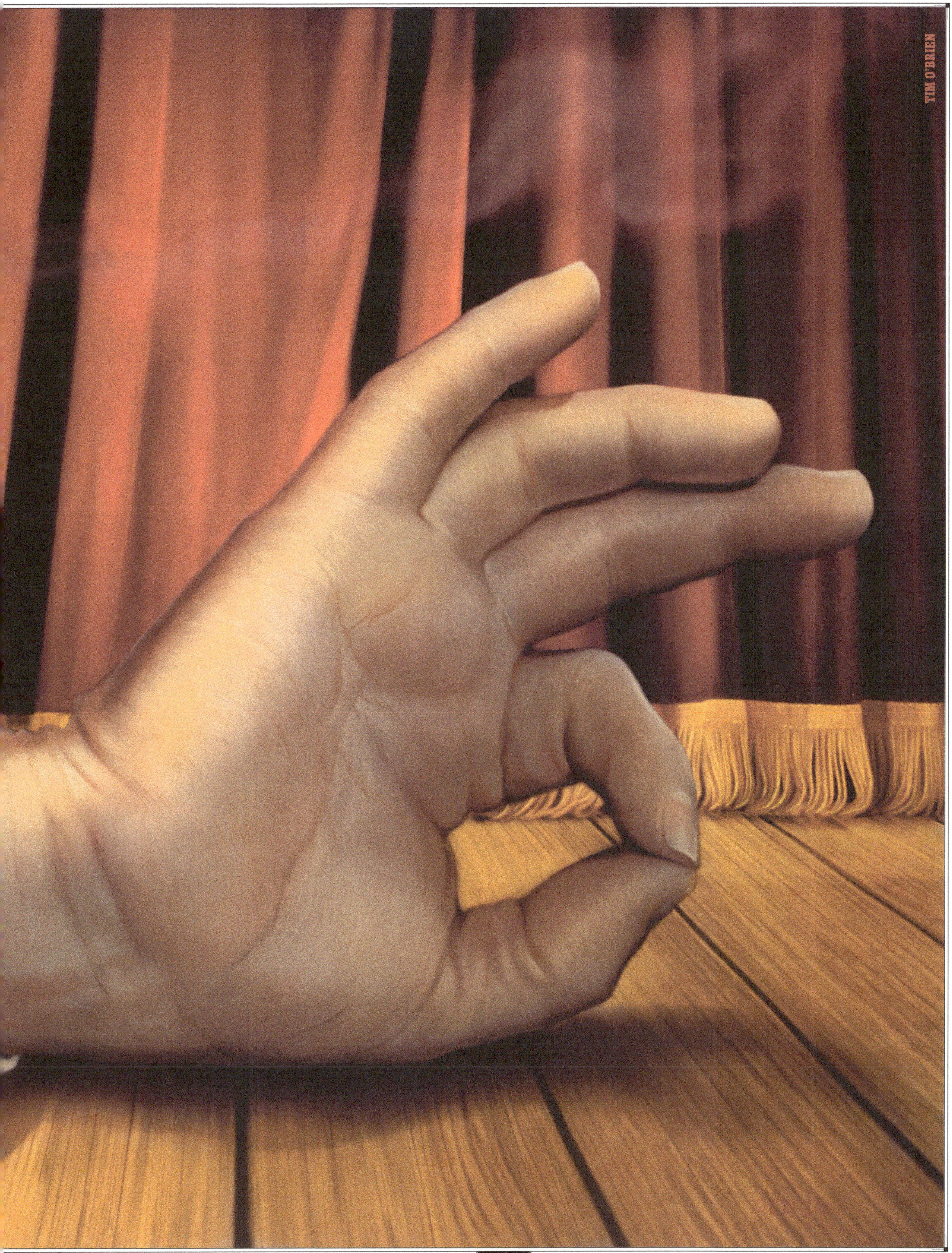
TIM O'BRIEN

She turned back, picking up her purse from the table. "Thank you for keeping us safe," she said to him.

"Thank you, ma'am," he said. Then, as if unwilling to surrender this vague intimacy between them, he added, "Flight surgeon?" He was looking at the badge upon her breast.

She gave him a look to suggest that, while she was proud of her service, she was not given to speaking of it. "Flight nurse," she said.

Standhope nodded. "SEACOPS," he said. "USS *Ardent*. And the *Dextrous*." He looked around at the Magic Kingdom. "In another life."

Molly felt her heart pounding in her breast. She wasn't entirely sure what sea cops were. Some kind of naval police, probably?

"Well," she said, "all ashore that's going ashore." She turned swiftly—too swiftly. A frisson of pain shot up from the inner socket encasing her thigh stump, and she cried out, "Fuck," a phrase that was not exactly on-brand.

"Ma'am?" said Standhope.

She moved away from him, trying to resist the impulse to run. Ahead of them was the train station, the old steam locomotive puffing happily away. Beyond that, Main Street. She wanted to look back. It was ironic that she'd got all the way through security only to nearly blow it at the last minute.

Back at the security station, Officer Standhope looked after Molly as she moved off into the crowd. He rubbed his chin. Then he went back to the computer screen and looked at the x-ray image again. Ms. Hernandez pointed at the screen with a pencil again. "This is what I was looking at," she said.

"The leg?" he said.

"No," she said, with irritation. "This thing. Hidden inside it."

When she had been raising the kids with Louise, the operating profanity had been *Oh for*. It was short, of course, for Oh for fuck's sakes, or even, Oh for the love of fuck. They'd agreed they weren't going to swear in front of the children, though, so *Oh for* became the go-to. Luke and Patrick had used it when they were toddlers, without having a clue that it was short for anything. In the same way Louise, her ex, had used "Sugar Honey Ice Tea," an Oklahomaism. They'd been married for almost twenty years before Molly realized that it was a way of spelling out "shit."

They'd been here once, maybe '98 or '99, Louise and the boyos, and they'd taken on the park like they were storming the beaches at Normandy. They arrived at rope drop, screamed toward Space Mountain, then got themselves over to Thunder Mountain Railroad right after. The park had started to fill up by mid-morning, but there was still time to check off Splash Mountain, Pirates of the Caribbean, and the Haunted House before lunch. She remembered the boys starting to flag after that, a complication that wasn't eased by the fact that they'd somehow strayed into a section of the park where the only thing to eat was turkey legs. Patrick, eight years old, had wanted to know, where's the rest of the turkey? Is it walking around with a leg like you, Daddy? Everyone thought this was hilarious, a turkey with a prosthethic limb. A paragobbler.

Louise had advocated a quick retreat after that, given that they'd checked off all the "A" rides, and the boyos were strangely fine with that, especially since she promised to bring them back for the fireworks. Molly—Mark, then—had been quietly pissy about not being able to take in the tackier rides which she actually loved most of all—the Carousel of Progress, Bear Country Jamboree, and dear god, the Enchanted Tiki Room. Still, it was not possible to be a connoisseur of kitsch if you hadn't developed a taste for irony. Which the rest of her family had not.

Her own father had been irony-challenged as well. Back then, as a boy named Mark, she'd begged him to take the family to Orlando. But he'd dismissed Mark's plea, saying, That's a place for babies. When you grow up, you'll understand, the gravity of the world. That's what you need to respect.

The gravity of the world, young Mark had thought. It was a thing his father could perceive, and he could not, at least not yet. He'd hugged his father's leg. "When I grow up, I want to be like you," he said.

After Molly came out, after the divorce, after a judge had ruled that she had no parental rights at all, that she

"I knew from the moment our eyes met that you were the one I was going to settle for."

CERISE ZELENETZ

was, in fact, an ongoing threat to their well-being, well: she had some sense of it now, the gravity of the world. She was blocked from their Facebook pages, hadn't even laid eyes on her own sons in years. They'd be in their late twenties by now, maybe with families of their own. Had they brought their own sons to the Magic Kingdom in the years since? Had they paused before the silhouette of Splash Mountain and remembered the family they had been?

I didn't say it was your laughin' place, Brer Fox, I said it was *my* laughin' place.

Molly made her way down Main Street to the moat in front of Cinderella's Castle, where she sat down on a bench for a moment, catching her breath. Inside the socket her stump throbbed. She checked her watch. 9:30 AM.

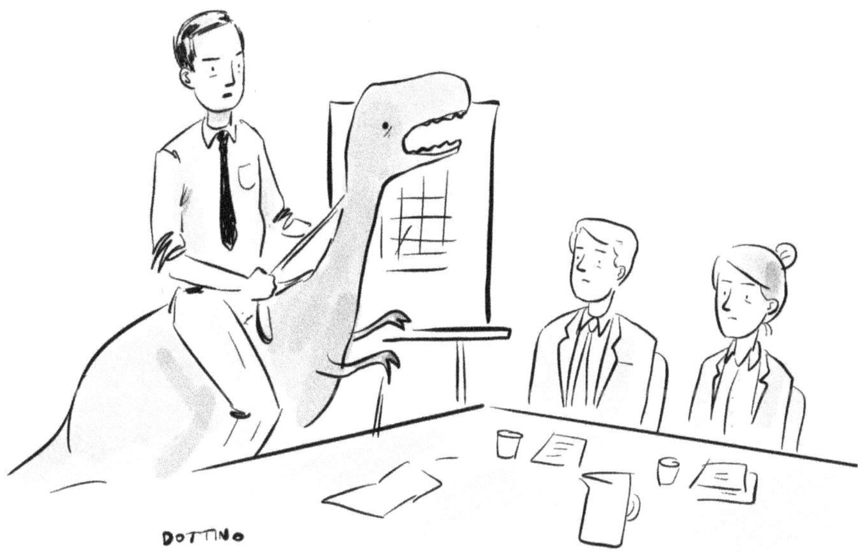
DOTTINO

"Before anyone says anything, this was built into the budget last year."

In a conference room one story directly below Main Street, Officer Standhope was reviewing the images from the x-rays with his immediate superior, Leo Livshits. Hernandez was there too. "A U.S. Navy officer, you say?" said Livshits. He was a large sweating man with a bald head and a grey mustache.

"She was wearing dress blues," said Standhope. "Flight nurse."

"Can I see the footage from the camera?" said Livshits.

"Here you go," said Hernandez. They all looked at the wall monitor, where the black-and-white video of Molly O'Carragain moving through the security line played. Livshits watched as Standhope looked into her purse with a flashlight, then rolled it through the x-ray. The woman moved through the portal, then paused as the alarm went off.

Livshits rubbed his eyes. "I'm not seeing it," he said.

"Well," said Standhope. "It's right there, in the leg."

"Yeah, I see that," he said. "It's a shadow, shaped like a sidearm. But it's probably bullshit. I'm thinking it's bullshit."

"Should we—" said Standhope. "Take her in?"

"That'd look great," said Livshits. "Hauling in a vet. Correction—a wounded vet. Because of some bullshit… *penumbra*. A penumbra of a shadow of an emanation, isn't that what they call it?"

"Sir," said Hernandez. "I'm thinking of the potential risks here—"

"I know what you're thinking," said Livshitz. "I just—" He ran his fat hand over his bald head again, from crown to chin. He sighed. "All right, fine. Bring her in. But do it with respect. You respect the hell out of her."

Standhope was staring at the screen with a strange expression.

"What?" said Livshits.

"She's a strange looking woman, isn't she?"

Molly stood before the waters surrounding Tom Sawyer Island. A ferryboat was churning away from her, a calliope puffing steam in the bright sunshine and playing "In the Good Old Summertime." In the distance to her right was the Haunted House, standing on its bluff overlooking the river. To the left was the promenade along the waters, the Diamond Horseshoe restaurant, the Country Bears, the Pecos Bill Tall Tale Inn. Somewhere beyond all that was Frontierland.

Another ripple of pain shot up her right leg. Yeah, Molly thought to herself. And when did surprise set in, exactly? There's a reason it doesn't sit right, given the alterations she'd had to make in order to sneak in the Glock. She found a bench.

A family walked by her, a pair of fat parents and four resentful children, all six of them eating turkey legs. A teenage daughter sucked on a pink slushie. Two of the children—twin boys, Molly figured—were wearing Hooters T-shirts. The father was wearing one of those Make America Great Again hats. She felt the rage seething within her.

There was a loud blast from the riverboat, startling everyone on shore, and the girl with the slushie dropped it on the sidewalk, where it exploded pinkly in every direction. The other members of her family burst into riotous laughter, like this was the funniest thing they had ever seen. The girl, who couldn't have been older than fourteen, stood there with her turkey leg, tears quivering in her eyes.

"Womp womp," said the dad.

A dufus paused before her. He was wearing camouflage, his T-shirt and his pants and his hat. His beer belly spewed over his belt, like a huge loaf of rising dough. By his side was a young boy, about eight, wearing a shirt with wide blue-and-white horizontal stripes.

"Thank you for your service," said the dad. The boy cowered behind the father's leg, viewing Molly with an expression of fear and awe.

She sat there, wondering what the proper response could be. You're welcome? It made her feel self-conscious about the whole ruse, and for an instant it occurred to her to come clean. Listen, she might say. I just borrowed

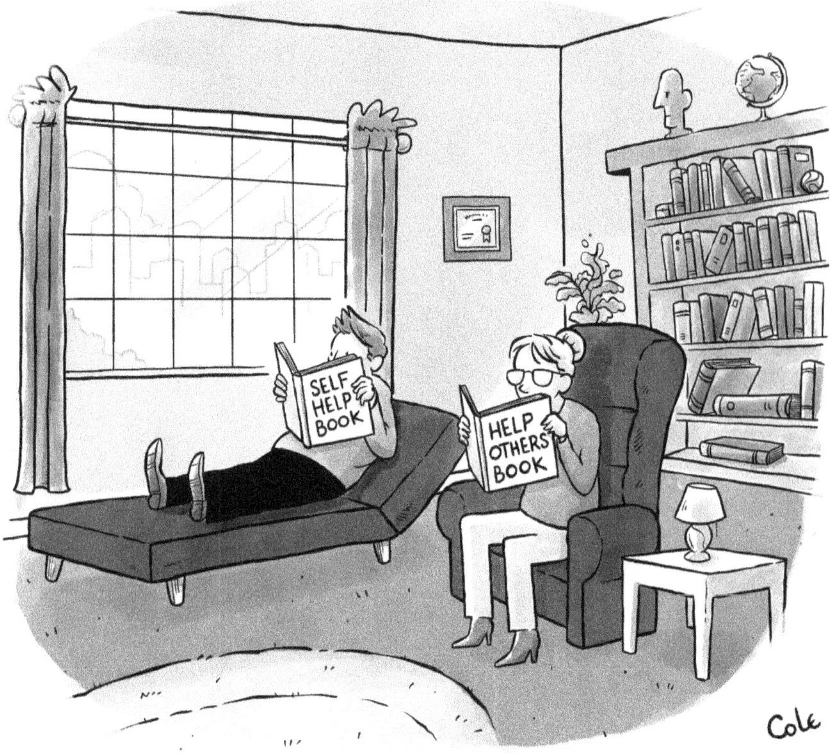
SELF HELP BOOK
HELP OTHERS BOOK
Cole

this uniform from my friend Coop. I figured it'd make them less likely to stop me at security. Truth is, I was never in the service. They wouldn't even let me serve, to tell you the truth, even if I volunteered. Or at least they wouldn't if Agent Orange gets his way, the unbearable, poisonous fuck.

But of course, it wasn't possible to say any of this. She just nodded somberly.

Molly figured that the dufus, along with his spawn, would be on their way after this, but the man just continued to stand there hunkering, while the child peered at her as if through a periscope. She tried to imagine the logic of the crap the man told himself to ease his conscience. After all, that's what everyone kept saying we needed to do, to open up our hearts and understand the disaffection of the rural white voter. But it seemed hopeless. She'd come from a Republican family, and the general idea of lower taxes, greater personal responsibility, smaller government—she understood the appeal of these things, as ideas. But how did we get from there to—*this place?*

"How'd you lose the leg?" the dufus enquired. The boy looked at his father, aware, even at his tender age, what an awful thing this was to ask another human being.

"Daaad," he said, in a stage whisper. "Let's go."

She'd rehearsed an answer before embarking on this mission, something about an IUD in Fallujah. I was out with a convoy, securing the perimeter, when suddenly—

IED, actually. Not an IUD. An improvised something device. As opposed to an Intra-Uterine Device. Which, as it turns out, was also something she'd never had. On account of not having a uterus, and stuff.

"Hey, you know what," Molly said, and suddenly stood up. "It's none of your business."

"Whoa," said the dufus. The boy retreated into himself, as if this was exactly what he'd foreseen. "I'm sorry, ma'am. I was just—"

"I said it's none of your fucking business," Molly snapped, and walked swiftly away from him, or as swiftly as she could with the pegleg. Out on the lagoon, the Mark Twain steamboat chugged toward Tom Sawyer Island.

The dufus stood there watching her go. Something about the woman in the uniform felt—off.

Two people, a man and a woman, rushed toward the bench where the officer had been sitting. They wore blue-grey uniforms with badges over the left breast and the Disney "D" logo on the right sleeve. Black caps with visors. They looked around, a little confused. One of them, a woman with a badge that read HERNANDEZ, turned to the dufus. "Excuse me sir," said she. "I don't suppose you've seen—?"

"Navy officer?" he replied. "Woman with a pegleg?"

"Yeah," said Standhope. "Was she just here?"

"Walked off that way," said the dufus, pointing toward Adventureland. His son appeared to be mentally crawling into an invisible cave. "What'd she do?"

"Nothing, sir," said Officer Hernandez. "We just want to talk to her."

"Well you should," said the dufus. "She's bats." He looked at his son. "Don't you think she was bats, Bruce?"

Bruce looked at the cops, and then at his father. "Yes," he said. "She was scary."

"Bats and scary," said Standhope. "How exactly?"

"I was just talking to her," said the dufus. "She used some language."

Hernandez was talking into a walkie-talkie she'd removed from her belt. "What do you see on the cameras?" she said. "Over."

She listened as Livshits replied.

"They get like that," said the dufus. "My son."

"We gotta go," said Hernandez.

"Your son?" said Standhope, looking at Bruce.

"My other son," said the dufus. "Post-traumatic stress. From the war." He shook his head. "It's like somebody took my boy away and gave me back some whole other person."

Bruce hung his head in shame, as if the some whole other person his father had been given was himself, rather than a transformed version of his older brother. It was clear enough that the father, given the choice, would have traded the young son in a heartbeat for an unharmed version of the older one.

"I'm sorry, sir," said Standhope.

"We gotta go," said Hernandez.

"You take care, sir," said Standhope.

"Yeah, okay," said the dufus, as the officers turned away and moved swiftly toward Adventureland. He looked down at Bruce, who was now inexplicably crying.

"Oh for God's sakes, what the hell are you crying about."

"I'm not," Bruce wept.

"Hey," he shouted after the cops. "Hey! What'd she do?"

Molly, sitting on a stall in the ladies' room halfway between the Tortuga Tavern and the Pirates League, had the leg off now and was removing the gun from the flexible inner socket. It was a Glock G42 Flat Dark Earth 380, with a 6+1 mag and a 3.25 inch barrel. She pulled out the magazine, then clicked it back into place. From the stall next to her came the sound of a flush, and for a moment Molly feared that the unmistakable sound of a Glock mag might have given her neighbor the willies, but a moment later she heard the stranger washing her hands in the sink, and someone else entered the stall next door. She could see a pair of shoes—sensible mom shoes, worn down trainers, exactly the kind of footwear popular with the suburban ladies who had helped deliver us to this hell-hole in the first place. Molly tried to imagine these people going into the voting booth, and weighing their choice: on the one hand, the first female president, a person arguably more experienced in public service than any previously nominated candidate, someone who would protect abortion rights, and health care, and the integrity of the Supreme Court. On the other hand, Agent Orange, this giant idiot moron. *Hmm*, said the mom, *O I can't choose. I guess I'll have to go with—Agent Orange!*

From the stall beside hers came the sound of agitated flushing. Molly aimed the muzzle of the Glock at the divider, right about the place where Mom Shoes was tidying up. There should be a sign, she thought. *Please do not flush country down toilet. Use the voting booths provided.*

Molly slipped the Glock into her purse and re-affixed the leg. As she did this, she tried to imagine the conversation she'd be having in the aftermath. Was it a political statement, they'd want to know. Something about the trans military ban, maybe? Or the ruling in the Masterpiece Cake case? Was it the Kavanaugh nomination? Or was it something more personal—maybe the memory of having been here before, with the family you had lost?

But it was none of these things, or none of them alone, in any case. In the end, it was because the land she once had known and loved had been taken from her, and transformed into a seething, turgid, selfie-taking, twitter-tweeting, effluvium-spewing sewer culvert.

That's why I shot him, she would say. I was trying to encourage everyone to be nice.

Molly was moving swiftly now. She walked past Pirates of the Caribbean on her right, the Enchanted Tiki Room on her left, the Magic Carpets of Aladdin dead ahead. The crowds thinned out in front of the Tiki Room, but it was still a hot day full of drained Americans. She had a quick memory of taking her boys through Pirates of the Caribbean years ago, how frightened they'd been of the room full of burning buildings. That little dog with the keys to the dungeon in its mouth, the jailed buccaneers praying they could coax it closer before they were consumed in flames. Then, they rounded the corner, and there it was, the ornate pirate ship, like something from a dream.

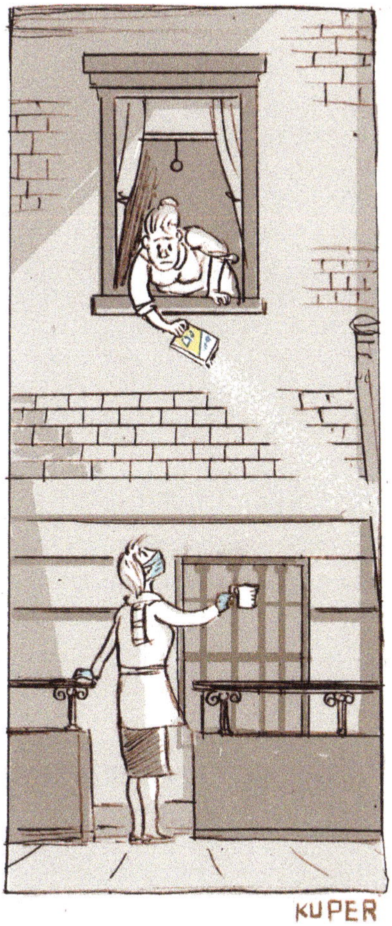
KUPER
"Perhaps there's another way I can safely borrow a cup of sugar."

She wondered what her sons were like now. It was not impossible they had sons of their own. What had her grandchildren been told? Yes, you had a grandfather, but he died. Something like this, she imagined. This is what cis people were like: it was easier to tell people you were dead than trans. Because death, in this view, at least came without shame. Whereas.

On her right now: the Swiss Family Treehouse. On her left: some kind of cafeteria. Just beyond this: the Sunshine Tree Terrace, where people in shorts were eating orange soft-serve ice cream. Now she came to the bridge above the lagoon and the sign above it reading ADVENTURELAND. She left this all behind. This took her to a square on the outskirts of the center pavilion, the Cinderella castle surrounded by gardens. There was a wire running to the castle, if you looked carefully, and it was upon this that the cast member portraying Tink would fly, once the sun went down. By then, she reckoned, she'd be in custody. Or, you know.

Molly took a left, the shortcut across the turgid Adventureland estuary, and followed the lagoon back toward Liberty Square. Dead ahead: Sleepy Hollow, with its funnel cakes, waffles, and sandwiches made from ice cream cookies shaped like a decapitated cartoon villain.

In the far distance, perched upon its bluff, were the towers of the Haunted Mansion. She remembered that song, "Grim Grinning Ghosts," on endless loop inside the ride, and how young Patrick had sat next to her in the hearse-car, his hands clamped over his face for the duration. You said it was going to be funny, he'd wept, afterwards.

Shrouded in a daft disguise, they pretend to terrorize.

Molly O'Carragain reached into her purse and felt the cool steel of the Glock, and gently clicked off the safety.

"I didn't get a good look at her," said a severe-looking woman, like the wife in the painting of the farmer with the

Social Distancing for sardines.

Social Distancing for Peas.

Social Distancing for shish kebab.

pitchfork. "I was already on my way out. All I saw was she was tall."

"This was how long ago?" said Standhope. They were in a cluster in front of the rest rooms in Adventureland.

"Like, a minute," said the farmer's wife. "She's probably still in there!"

"Okay," said Hernandez. "We're going in."

"I'll wait here," said Standhope.

Hernandez, halfway to the entrance, turned back. "The hell you will, come on, let's go!"

"I don't think it's appropriate," Standhope said. "Men in the ladies room!"

"The fuck, come on!"

"I'm not going in there!" Standhope said, more firmly.

"We have an armed suspect!" said Hernandez. "I think that trumps—"

"Armed?" said the farmer's wife. "What do you mean, armed?"

Standhope ground his teeth. "Fine," he said, and followed Hernandez into the den of pleasure.

"Did he say armed?" said a thin man to the farmer's wife.

"Sorry, ladies!" said Standhope, in a loud voice. He hunkered near the sinks with his weapon drawn. "Just keeping everybody safe!"

A woman came out of a stall. She had ornate tattoos on both arms, from shoulder to wrist. Swastikas crawled along her biceps. She sudsed up her hands and rinsed them, and then placed them beneath a high-powered hand dryer, this being the most efficient way of preventing the spread of disease.

Hernandez went from stall to stall, looking underneath the doors at the shoes of women. "Shit," she said.

Standhope waited uncomfortably by the sinks. He thought back to his days on the USS *Ardent*, a whole ship populated only by men. That was a different world than this. It smelled different in ladies rooms. There was something acrid and salty in the air. What was it—the smell of iron?

"We've lost her," said Hernandez. Sweat was trickling down her temples, plastering her black curly hair to her skin.

"Do we know that?" said Standhope.

"Everybody here," said Hernandez, "has two feet."

"Maybe that's just what she wants us to think," said Standhope.

Hernandez looked at her partner. "Are you all right?" she said. "Seriously?"

"I don't know," said Standhope. "I'm confused."

"Livshits, Hernandez," she said into her radio. "She's given us the slip again."

There was some swearing from the other end. Then Livshits said, "I'm giving you ten minutes to find her, then we're going Code Nine."

"Is that really necessary?" said Standhope. "Maybe we could just—"

"What do you see on the monitors?" Hernandez asked. "Talk to me."

Standhope looked out the door of the women's room at the Magic Kingdom beyond. He remembered standing on the deck of the Ardent, nothing to see in every direction except the Indian Ocean. The bow rose and fell.

He tried to put himself in this woman's shoes. Shoe. What were her intentions? If the goal was to create the greatest amount of mayhem, where would you go? And what would you do? From the distance Standhope heard the laughter of children. The steam whistle on the Mark Twain blasted into the morning air.

"Say that again," said Hernandez, into her radio. "She's where?"

The first thing Molly saw as she moved through the lobby was that same dufus from the lagoon having some sort of argument with his son. She didn't want to get too close, in case her indiscreet reply to him had somehow aroused his suspicions. But even at this distance, you could see the child didn't want to go in. The dad was adamant, though, even as the child squatted down on the floor and tried to escape his father's grasp. I don't care, said the man. We're going.

Molly moved on into the crowd, although admittedly it was pretty hard to blend in anywhere, being six feet tall, and walking on a peg leg, and wearing a naval officer's uniform. Of course, people couldn't see the pegleg unless they noticed the space between her shoe and the bottom of her trouser-cuff, where the shaft that held the force sensor was just barely visible above the dynamic foot.

The air was full of sleepy conversations; this was not the place you went when you first came into the park. This was something you did toward the end, after your will to live had been sapped by the long lines and the turkey legs, and all you wanted was to sit in some anonymous silence.

Molly passed into the theatre and took a seat on the aisle, not too close, but not too far either. Her stump ached, but then that was to be expected with all the custom alterations she'd had to make to the socket in order to smuggle the Glock through security. Still, the pain that she was feeling seemed to go deeper, right to the bone. It wasn't a good sign.

Before her was the blue curtain with the presidential seal projected upon it. An announcer spoke in a reverential and stentorian tone: "This program is dedicated to the memory of Walt Disney. In 1971, his love for America inspired the creation of the Hall of Presidents. A place to celebrate the optimism and good will he saw at the heart of the American story."

The curtains parted. Fog and smoke drifted across the stage. There was a painting of what looked like George Washington planting the Betsy Ross flag atop of Iwo Jima. Now there was a new announcer, a woman. "It is 1783. The smoke is clearing from the Revolutionary War." And so on. Molly just shook her head, and thought about poor old Walt. He got cancer, too, died sometime in the 60s, the Johnson years, she figured. The Watusi. The Twist. El Dorado.

From behind her, she heard a strange sound, like weeping. At first it was suppressed, then it swelled into something more like open sobbing. "Quit it," said another voice, and she didn't have to turn around to see. "I swear to God. I'll give you something to cry about."

For a while Molly just sat there, listening to the twin sounds: the child behind her weeping, the announcer narrating a gussied-up version of American history from the Revolution to the Civil War. It was like listening to a radio stuck between stations. Jesus Christ, she thought. Just like my own miserable life.

She felt the gun in her purse, and thought of Coop. I am Molly O'Carragain, she thought. And I am an instrument for the love of God.

Now the curtains parted, and there was Abe Lincoln, sitting in a chair, a wooden version of the marble throne he sat upon in his Memorial. He stood up. The president wore a long coat that fell nearly to his knees. There were four buttons on each side of the coat. He also had a loose bow tie, and a vest. "Four score and seven years ago," he said. "Our forefathers brought forth upon this continent, a new nation, conceived in Liberty, and dedicated to the proposition that all men are created equal."

"And women!" someone shouted, from the back of the hall.

"Sshh," said someone else.

"Jesus H. Christ," said the dufus behind her. "It's gonna be like that now?"

After the Gettysburg Address, Lincoln sat back down, and the curtains were

............◆............

> She felt the gun in her purse. I am Molly O'Carragain, she thought. And I am an instrument for the love of God.

............◆............

drawn again. Then time speeded up. Images flashed across the screen of the country's growing prosperity. Teddy Roosevelt waved at a crowd. The pistons of locomotives raced forward and back. Miners panned for gold. Molten steel poured from buckets in a foundry and sparks flew in the air. Then FDR allowed as how there was nothing to fear etc etc. Now it was VE Day in Times Square. And seconds later: holy cow, we were going to the Moon! Louie Armstrong played the trumpet. Jack Kennedy, in his lovely tails, said, "Ask not," etc. Martin Luther King appeared in shirt sleeves. Jimmy Carter stood between Anwar Sadat and Menachem Begin, and everyone shook hands all around. There was Reagan, and Clinton. The twin towers fell. Obama walked across the Edmund Pettus Bridge.

She thought about the passage of time, both its deadly protraction and its heartbreaking velocity. When her boys were small, she remembered that feeling—that each day took an eternity to pass. But the years had passed by like wind.

"Ladies and gentlemen, the Presidents of the United States of America," said the announcer, and the curtain rose again on the tableau of the forty-four robots gathered upon the stage. Some of them sat serenely in chairs, others stood around, clutching at their lapels. Everyone was winking and blinking.

Trump stood at the center of the stage, wearing a black suit and a blue and white diagonally striped tie. Lincoln sat in a chair next to him, and on the other side, Ulysses S. Grant. The presidents were gathered in little groups, arranged by chronology. The founding fathers—Washington, Adams, Jefferson, Madison, Monroe, were all stage left. As they were introduced, a small spotlight shone on their visages, and the robots looked duly humble. The other robots looked at them with deference.

The prewar presidents passed in a blur, most of them stage right. Lincoln glared at them: Jackson, van Buren, Harrison, Tyler, Polk, Taylor. Strangely, Millard Fillmore was standing nearly at center stage, behind Trump and Lincoln. Abe didn't turn around to look him in the eyes, or Franklin Pierce, either. You couldn't blame him—each one of those ignoramuses having done all they could to force the moment to its crisis.

Then James Buchanan, the old doughface. And finally, Abraham Lincoln, and as the name was spoken, Trump gestured with his left arm as if to say, *The Great Emancipator, amiright?*

Then it was on to Andrew Johnson, who was also nearly center stage, standing next to Buchanan, just over Trump's left shoulder.

Behind her, she heard the boy sobbing again. "You're crying at U.S. Grant now?" said the dufus. "Seriously?"

"That's not why," said the child.

The postwar presidents were all on the far right side of the stage, and the robots craned their neck to see. Hayes, Garfield, Arthur, Cleveland, Harrison, McKinley.

They had arrived in the 20th Century now, and Molly felt her heart pounding. *I'm really going to do this*, she thought. *It's all happening right now.*

Roosevelt, Taft, Wilson, Harding. There was a flash of light as doors opened at the back of the house, and two figures came down the aisles. They made their way to the front and shone their flashlights out into the audience. There was some muttering among the crowd at this. The flashlight played over Molly's face but they didn't see her, not yet anyhow. Coolidge, Hoover, FDR, Truman.

Molly looked around, wondering whether she should change the plan at the last second. Would it be so different if she spun around and took aim in a different direction? The flashlight played off of her face again, blinding her for a moment. "Hey, quit it!" shouted the dufus. "You're wrecking the whole show!"

Eisenhower, Kennedy, LBJ, Nixon, Ford, Carter. Now Reagan, the unbelievable idiot. The flashlight beam glanced across Molly's face again, and this time they froze upon her. Henandez shouted to Standhope. *We got her*, and the two of them moved quickly up the aisle toward her. "Ma'am," said Hernandez. Bush, Clinton, Bush, Obama. "Ma'am."

She stood up, took off the safety and aimed. Hernandez drew her weapon, and so did Standhope. The President began to speak. "I, Donald John Trump, do solemnly swear that I will faithfully execute—"

Molly pulled the trigger. It was louder than she thought. "—the office of President of the United States, and will, to the best of my ability—" He was still talking, although she noted that the Ulysses S. Grant's head was now hanging at a weird angle. *God dammit*, she thought. *After all this, I'm going to wind up shooting the wrong fucking robot.* Some smoke puffed from a hole in the general's neck.

The officers were almost upon her now. Molly shot again. "—defend the Constitution of—" She pulled off two more shots. Then there was a shot that did not come from her gun. The Trump robot wobbled. It raised one hand to its cheeks.

"—the United States. So help me God." Now people in the audience were screaming. A row of people off to the right rose to their feet.

They're actually shooting at me now, Molly wondered? Somehow, step by painful step, she had walked into this world. Well, fine, she thought. Screw it. Molly emptied the magazine, one gunshot after another echoing in the theatre. The robot President shook, like a can of paint in a mixer, and then all at once, Donald Trump's head fell off of his shoulders and rolled across the floor. Someone in the audience screamed. Someone else laughed, as if this was funny.

She felt the impact as Hernandez tackled her and crushed her to the floor. The Glock fell from her hands and skittered down the steps leading toward the proscenium. Standhope, out of breath, climbed on top of her and helped clamp her into a pair of handcuffs. Incredibly, the recorded part of the program was still going. "From the beginning," Trump's voice said, "it was the People who rose up to defend our freedoms."

"Everything's under control," Standhope said to the crowd. "Just a guest who's sick. We're going to take her to get help."

Molly, lying on the floor of the Hall of Presidents, felt the officer on her back. It reminded her of football practice, decades and decades ago, back when she'd been forced to play against her will. They made all the boys play, back in middle school. It was torture then, the incomprehensible signals being called, echoing inside her too-large helmet, followed a moment later by some stranger out of nowhere crushing her to the ground. Compared to that, this wasn't so bad. In fact, now that it was done, she felt nothing but a sense of calm.

"Suspect apprehended," Standhope was saying into his radio. "Situation under control."

Hernandez was helping her to her feet now. "Can I ask you something?" she said, looking at Molly carefully. "What's this all about? All this work to shoot a robot? Seriously?"

But Molly just thought, *Sic semper culus!* Thus always to assholes!

Now that she was safely in custody, the other people in the theatre—those that had not fled after the firing of the shots—were watching her arrest with fascination, with expressions that—to be honest—were a lot more excited than they'd been during the introduction of James K. Polk. People were pulling out their phones to record the whole thing. Some, Molly realized, had been videotaping the show from the beginning. By nightfall, if everything went just so, she'd be internet-famous.

They started to escort her out of the theatre. But suddenly, there at her side was the small boy.

He went up to Molly and looked at her with a face of tragic longing. Her father shouted at him. "Get back here! Now!" But the child just stood there, tears shimmering in his eyes. Then he put his arms around her, and clutched on to Molly like she was someone he had lost. "Where's your mother?" Molly said. "What happened to her?"

Someone clapped, and the sound in the confused auditorium sounded like another gunshot.

Then other people started clapping, softly at first, then more loudly. A ripple of cheers broke out as the audience in the Hall of Presidents began to applaud. Molly felt a frisson of pain vibrate through her bones as she was escorted from the building like a hero. *God bless America!* someone shouted. *God bless the United States of America!*

The officers tried to move Molly toward the exit, but the aisles were now jammed with people shouting and waving their phones around and laughing and cheering with abandon. She thought, fleetingly, of her mother. But the greatest of these is love.

Molly looked down at the child still affixed to her leg, but it was not the face of young Bruce that she saw staring up at her now. It was her former self, young Mark, the child she once had been.

His young face was full of hope, full of an idealism and faith that the world had somehow not yet crushed.

"When I grow up," he said, "I want to be like you."

B

A GUIDE TO MASKED EMOTIONS VOL. 1

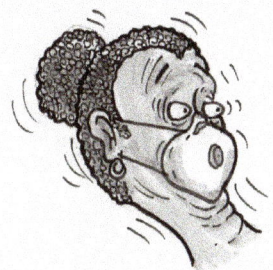
WAS THAT A SNEEZE???

WE'RE ALL GONNA DIE

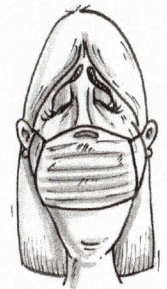
PROJECTING "PEACE TO ALL BEINGS" LIKE A JERK

GIMME ONE GOOD REASON TO REACH FOR MY PIECE

THESE MASKS ARE HOT AS BALLS

SUSPICIOUSLY REGARDING THE ANTI-VAXXERS NEXT DOOR

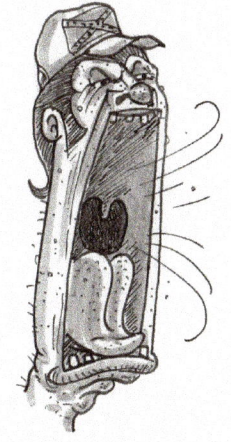
DEFIANTLY INHALING HIS FREEDOMS

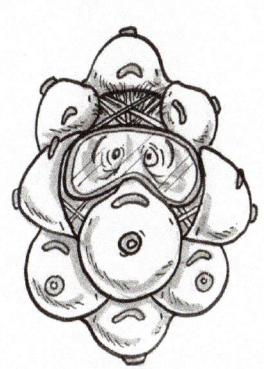
O.C.D. ISSUES IN OVERDRIVE

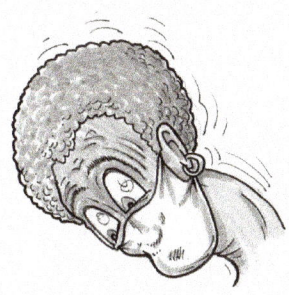
JUST STEPPED ON A RUBBER GLOVE

STILL CHECKING OUT EVERY FEMALE JOGGER

SIX FEET, PLAGUE RAT !!!

ACTUALLY, JUST ROBBING YOU

Les Dents de la Mer

A book by any other name…

"Well, what the hell are you going to call it?"
"*A Stillness in the Water*? I'm not sure."
"Not sure?" Tom Congdon, my brother Peter's editor at Doubleday, was beginning to run out of patience. "The book goes to press in half an hour."
"Let's keep thinking."

Tom tried to stay calm. He and Peter had worked for months through the birthing of a novel about a fish, fought off a less-than-sterling first draft and persevered right up to the final moment without giving up. But here, in a Midtown steakhouse, the fuse was lit, and he and his young author were about to be hoist with their own petard if they couldn't come up with a catchy title.

Thirty minutes.

Tom sipped his drink. And Peter thought.

The whole thing had started, as most panics do, innocuously. Several years earlier Congdon had taken a 32-year-old ex-presidential speechwriter to lunch and popped the usual question: "Got any ideas for a novel?"

Peter had been bouncing around, doing a variety of jobs since Lyndon Johnson had turned the keys over to Richard Nixon's gang. "I've got two outlines I like," Peter said. One was about pirates in the modern-day Caribbean; and the other was about a giant shark which establishes residence around a beach community. Although his wife, Wendy, had gently said she thought that a story about a giant shark was "a bit far-fetched," he still clung to the possibility.

Congdon didn't leap at either option—but there were reasons to take a small gamble on the young writer. Before writing speeches and toasts for The leader of the free world, Peter had been the first TV editor at *Newsweek* and had published a nonfiction book and a children's book. He was now freelancing for a collection of reputable newspapers, magazines and TV stations.

And, for what it was worth, Peter had a pedigree. Our grandfather was Robert Benchley who, if you're reading this magazine, needs no introduction. Our father, Nathaniel Benchley, was also a successful writer with dozens of books to his name, and a few movies to boot. His biggest hit had been a 1961 novel called *The Off-Islanders*, which was turned into the 1966 hit movie *The Russians Are Coming, The Russians Are Coming*.

Congdon thought it worth a modest advance to turn this latest Benchley loose upon the world of arts and letters. He offered the struggling writer $1,000 to produce the first few chapters about a ravenous, man-eating shark.

After several patient months waiting for…anything, Congdon let it be known that the chapters were due, or the advance should be returned. Unfortunately, nothing spends faster than a book advance in the hands of a growing family. In a panic, Peter went to work…and it all went wrong. Peter's upbringing had instilled in him a love of wordplay and sophisticated humor, neither of which was remotely appropriate for the job at hand: his first draft was half Melville-esque sea yarn, half Robert Benchley-esque diversion. Congdon's strong rejection produced an epiphany in Peter: "A funny thriller about a shark eating people is, I soon realized, a nearly perfect oxymoron."

Back to the typewriter Peter went and, after more than a year, the second draft turned out much better. So well, in fact, that Doubleday sent their salespeople out to book clubs and movie producers armed only with the first eight exciting pages. The clubs and producers were, as they say, hooked.

So, the book would at least be published. But Peter knew it had no chance of success. It was, after all, a first novel. And about a fish! Let's be real. Sure, the Benchleys were lucky—Robert had stumbled into success after success, being described once as "rather than a master of his own fate, he was more a stowaway aboard it." But surely there were limits, and as the clock wound down to zero, Peter saw those limits approaching. (There's a two-note phrase of John Williams' music that would be appropriate here, but it hadn't been written yet.)

The title had always been a problem. During the process of producing his "fish book," Peter and Wendy had endlessly noodled. Peter had a wealth of material inside him from

---

Nat Benchley *is a former performer/informer currently dividing his time between quarantine and sequestration.*

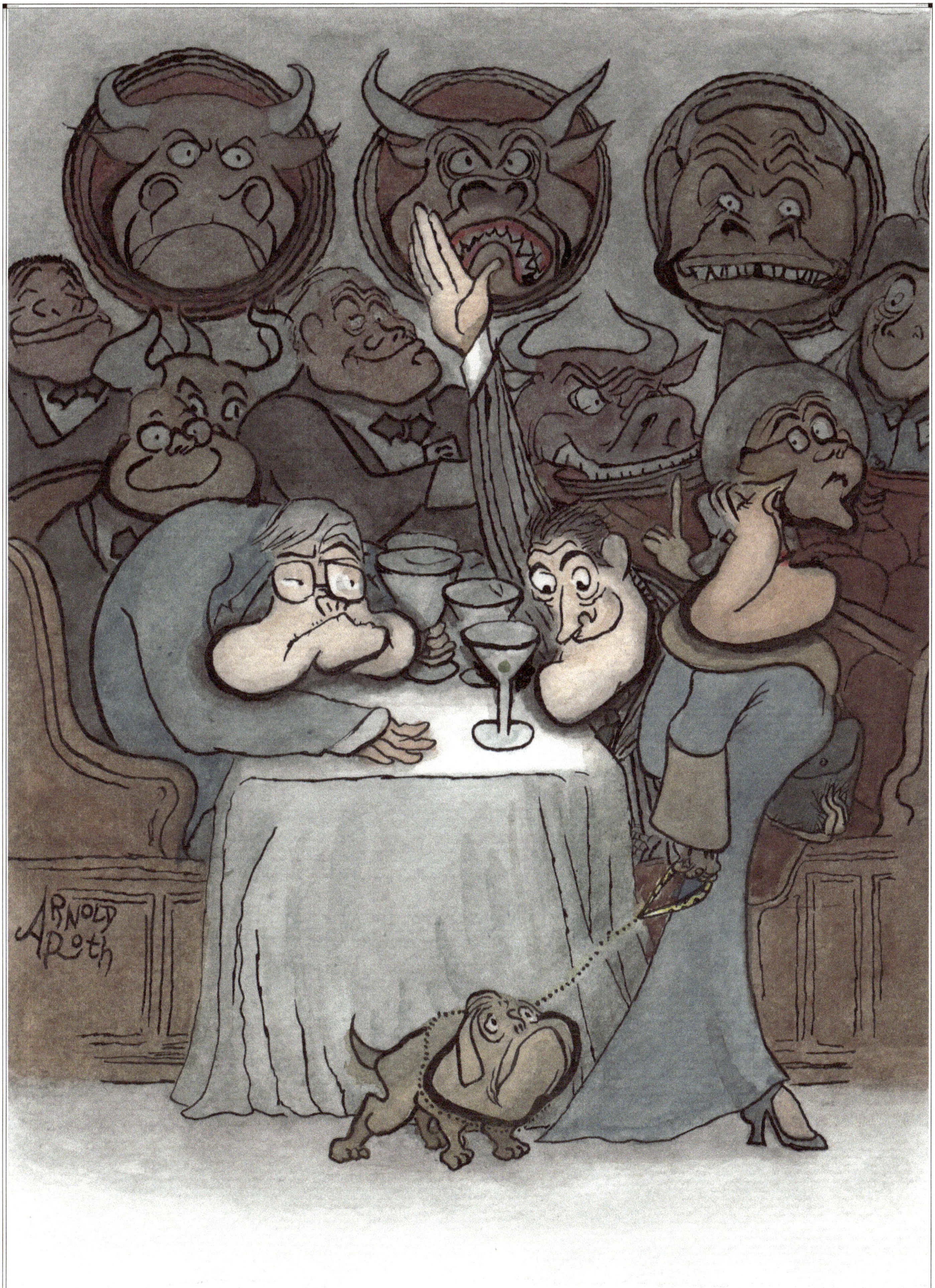
ARNOLD ROTH

growing up on the water in Nantucket, seeing that ominous fin cutting through the water, cleaning sharks' jaws on the roof of the garage…But what summed the book up? And what would sell?

Peter was fascinated by some of the names of the towns on the island, old Native American names like Squam; Shimmo; Madaket; Polpis; Miacomet; Siasconset. He began riffing on those. He also (by his own admission) concocted titles "reminiscent of French novels in vogue at the time, like *A Stillness in the Water* and *The Silence of Death*." Biblical references crept in, too: *Leviathan*, *Leviathan Rising* and *The Jaws of Leviathan*.

Totally frustrated, Peter turned to his father. After he heard the premise, Nathaniel suggested *Wha's That Noshin' on My Laig?* and (for the X-rated version) *Cunna Linga Here No Longa*.

On and on the search went. *White Death? The Jaws of Death. Summer of the Shark*. Which one was better? Are we getting anywhere? I don't think we're getting anywhere…

As the months rolled along with no title, Peter took solace in obscurity. Who cared what they called it? It was just a first novel, a throw-away, a warm-up. Nobody would read it. Then Tom told him that it was pre-selling at a furious pace, and the cold sweat began again. Friends were enlisted, and it became a community effort. Peter saved many pages of notes, scribbled in his and Wendy's handwriting: *Great White; White Night; Shimmo Night; Death in Shimmo; A Night in Shimmo; Death in Squam; Shimmo Bay; Dark Water/White Dark; The Shark of Shimmo; The Grinning Fish; The Visitor to Shimmo; Polpin Rock; The Beast of Shimmo; Squam Head; Moon's Neck; Shimmo White; Esau; Hooper/Clasper; Adrenalin; Peter Ginkel; Leviathan Rising; Throwback; The Coming; Horror; Haunt; The Fish; Phosphorescence; Looming; Clam Bay; Spectre; The Edge of Gloom; Maw; Endurance; Tumult; Shadow; The Survivor; The Unexplained; Penance; Hunger; Survival; Messenger; Dues; Ripple; Death From the Sea; Apparition; What Have We Done?; Stranger Summer; One Summer; Desserts; Tiburon* [the eventual title in Spanish]; *The White; Fluke; Monimoy; Requin; White; Why?; Quidnet; Off the Beach; Instinct; Arrival; Early Summer; Moon* (Town name); *Ravage; Warning; Despair; Shadows of Despair; Alarm; Beware; Giant; Portent; Menace; Scourge; Devastation; The Great Fish; A Question of Evil; Anthropophagus; Omnivore; Havoc; White Evil; White Menace; Jaws of Despair; Terror; Anguish; The Fish; In With Stillness; Amity; Hiram; Requiem White; Dread; Fury; Chill; Harpoon; A Dreadful Stillness; An elegant (splendid) presence; Man Eater; Out of the Stillness; An Awful Stillness; Leviathan; The Image of Evil; The Presence of Evil; Presence; Primeval; Infinite Evil; Primordial; Evil Infinite; Survival; Sacrifice; Vision; Brute White; Vengeance; A Question of Vengeance; Rollie; Tristram; The Scourge of Amity; Dreadful Silence; Jaws Over Amity; The Fish at Amity; Pisces Redux; Past…*

Nothing was sticking. After the first ten, it all sounded like mush. After the first thirty, it wasn't even English anymore.

And time was most definitely running short.

Congdon took Peter to lunch at The Dallas Cowboy steakhouse to put the figurative gun to his head and make him decide. Half-hour to lift-off. You can't print a book without a title.

In his own words, Peter described the lunch:

"Finally, when we had finished lunch and Tom had paid the check, I said, "Look, there's no way we're gonna agree on a title. There's only one word we agree on, so let's make that the title. Let's call it *Jaws*."

Tom thought for a moment, then agreed. "At least it's short."

I called my father and told him the title.

"What's it mean?" he asked.

"I have no idea," I said. "But at least it's short."

From this remove, with the benefit of not only hindsight but hysteria, it is hard to imagine any other title working. Or fitting as well on a T-shirt.

Sometimes desperation provides genius.

The old Benchley luck might have had something to do with it, too. **B**

T.Q. Chen's Quarantine Diary

Trapped in his Long Island City pad, art student ***Tianqi Chen*** *proves that boredom is a universal language.*

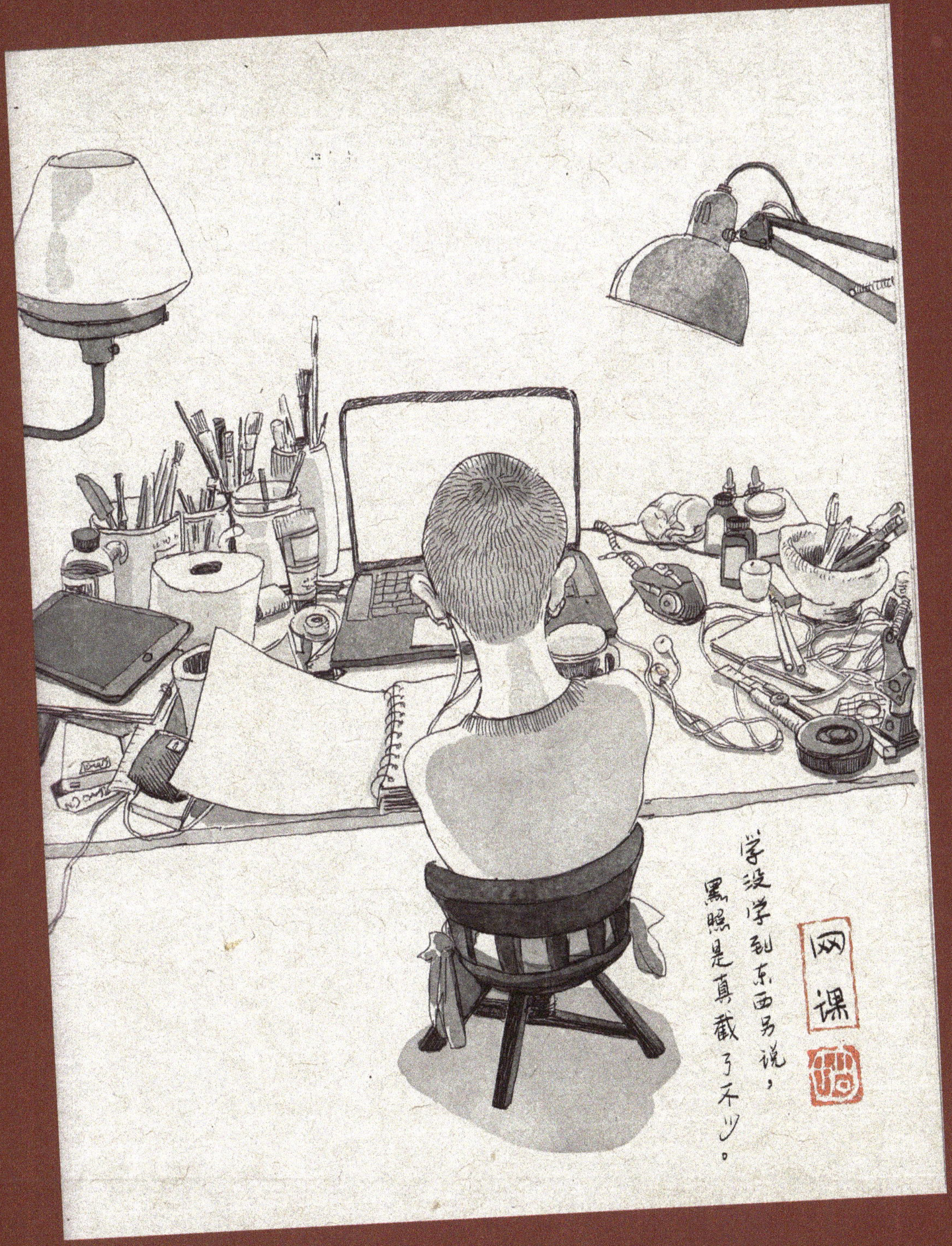
网课
学没学到东西另说，
黑照是真截了不少。

[translated from the Chinese]
"Zoom meeting. Got a lot of funny screenshots."

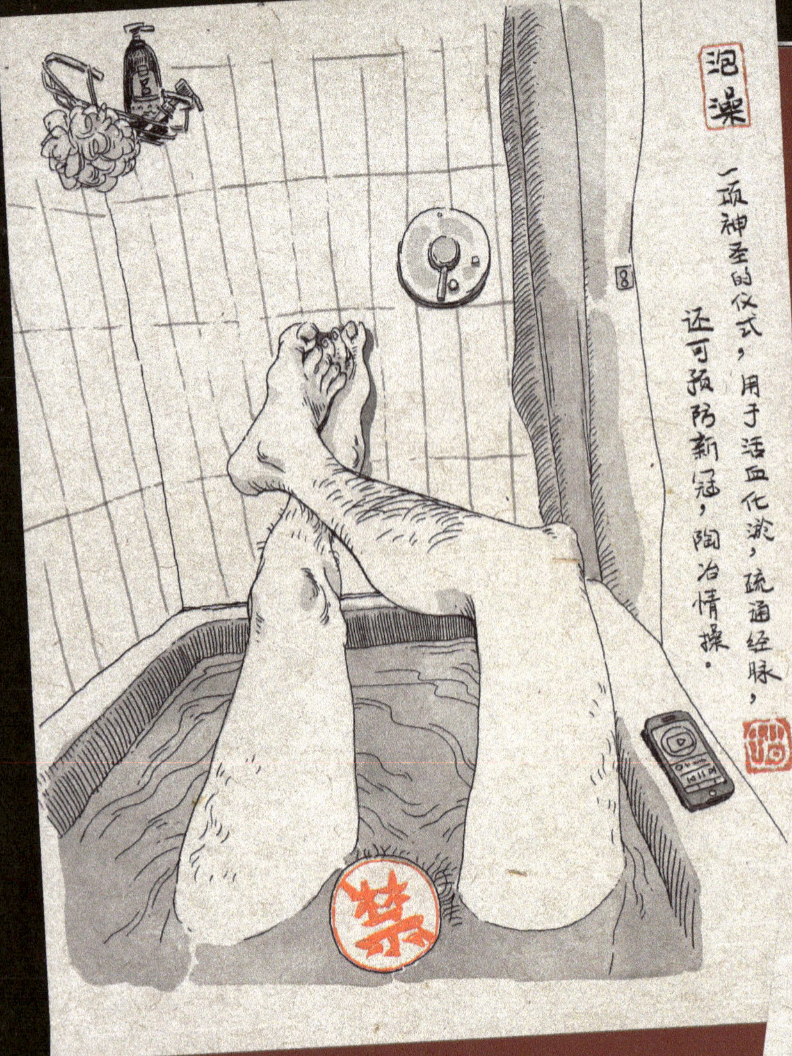
泡澡
一项神圣的仪式，用于活血化淤，疏通经脉，还可预防新冠，陶冶情操。
禁

"Bath time. A sacred ritual. Good for treating various diseases. Feeling holy every time I get out of the bathtub."

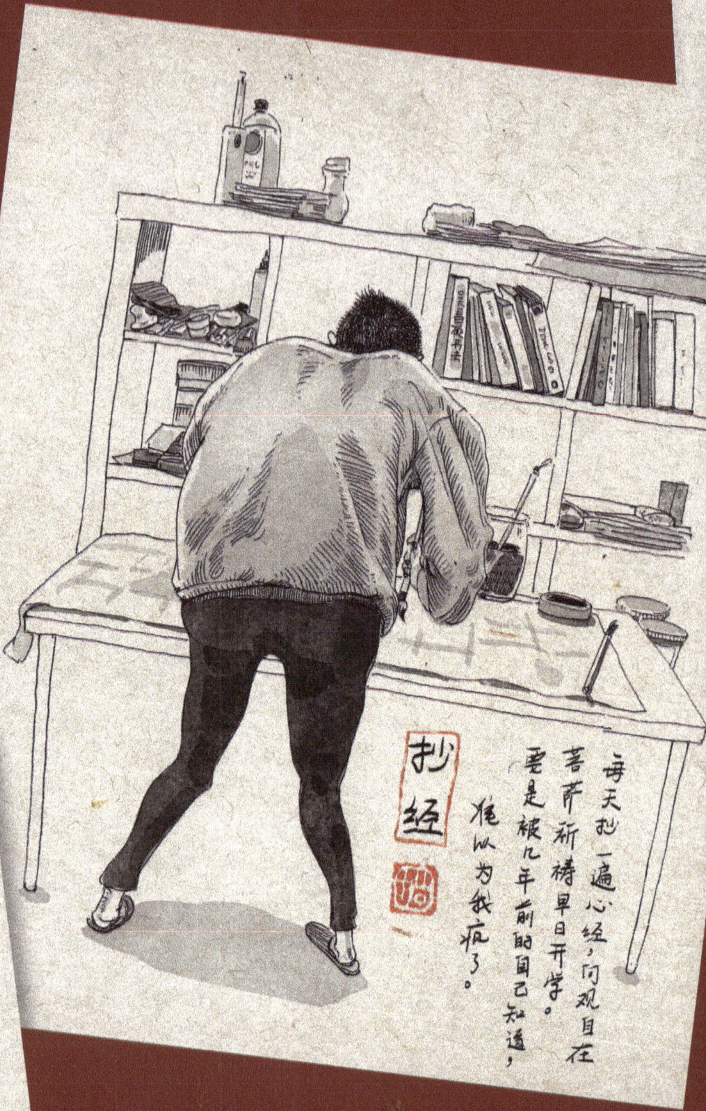
抄经
每天抄一遍心经，问观自在菩萨祈祷早日开学。要是被几年前的自己知道，准以为我疯了。

"I do the Xinjing calligraphy every day, and pray to the Buddha for school to open soon. Endless vacation is no fun anymore."

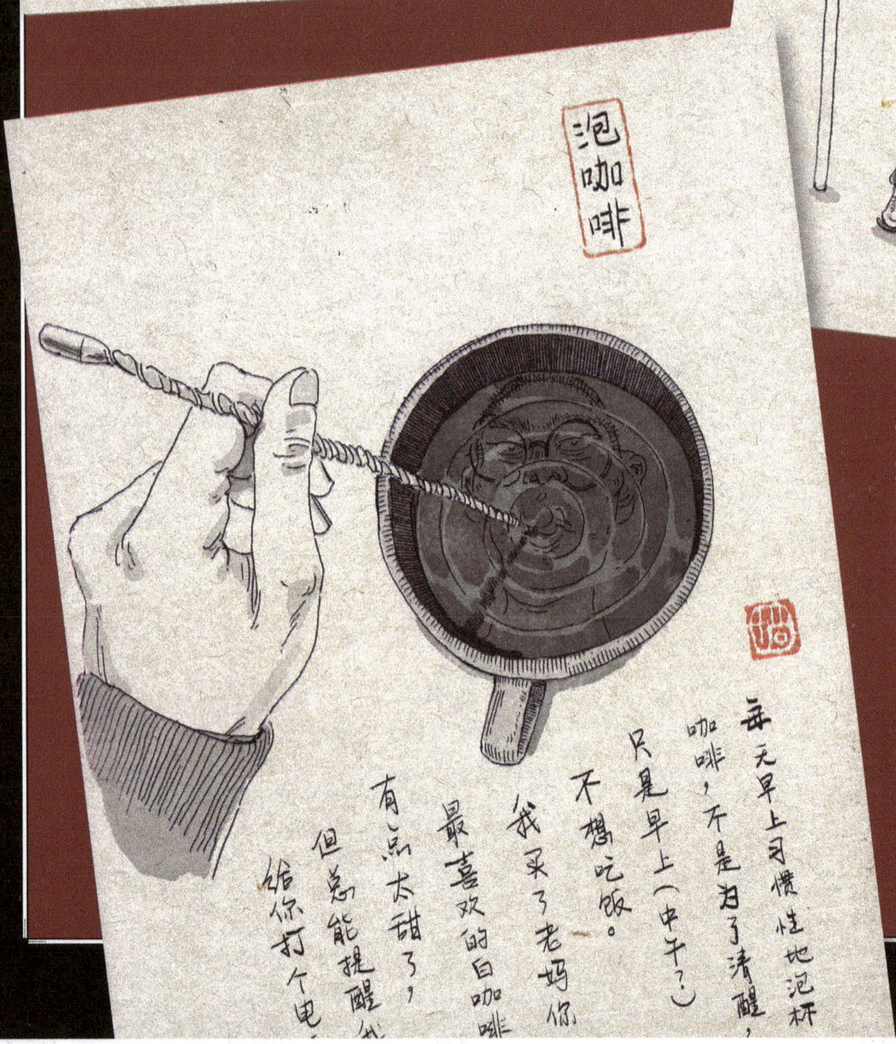
泡咖啡
每天早上习惯性地泡杯咖啡，不是为了清醒，只是早上（中午？）不想吃饭。我买了老妈你最喜欢的白咖啡，有点太甜了，但总能提醒
给你打个电

"Coffee time. I bought Mom's favorite white coffee, not because it tastes good, but it reminds me of giving her a phone call."

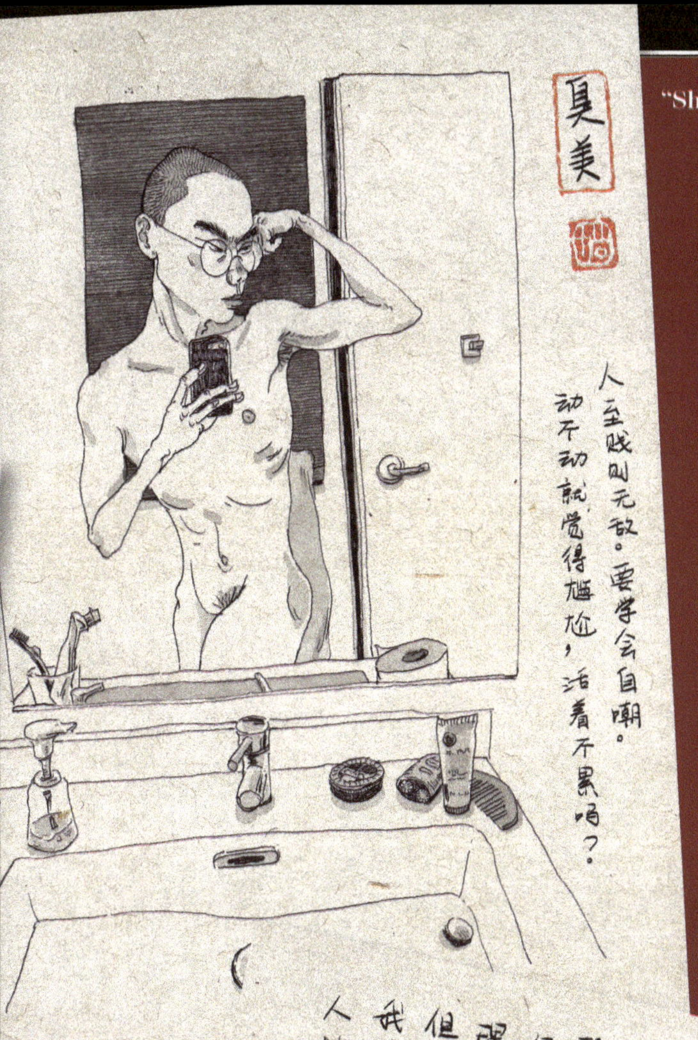
臭美
人至贱则无敌。要学会自嘲。
动不动就觉得尴尬，活着不累吗？

"Shameless selfie. Don't you get tired of always acting serious?"

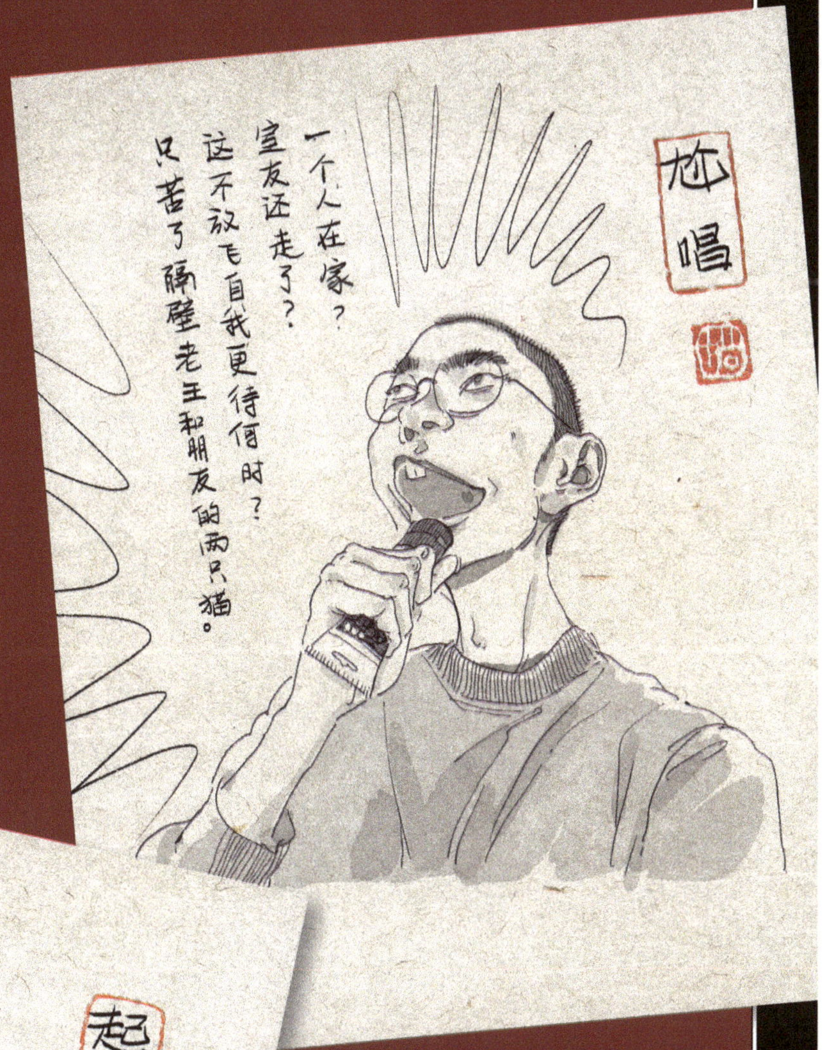
独唱
一个人在家？
室友还走了？
这不放飞自我更待何时？
只苦了隔壁老王和朋友的两只猫。

"Singing alone. As a Karaoke nerd, staying home is such a torture."

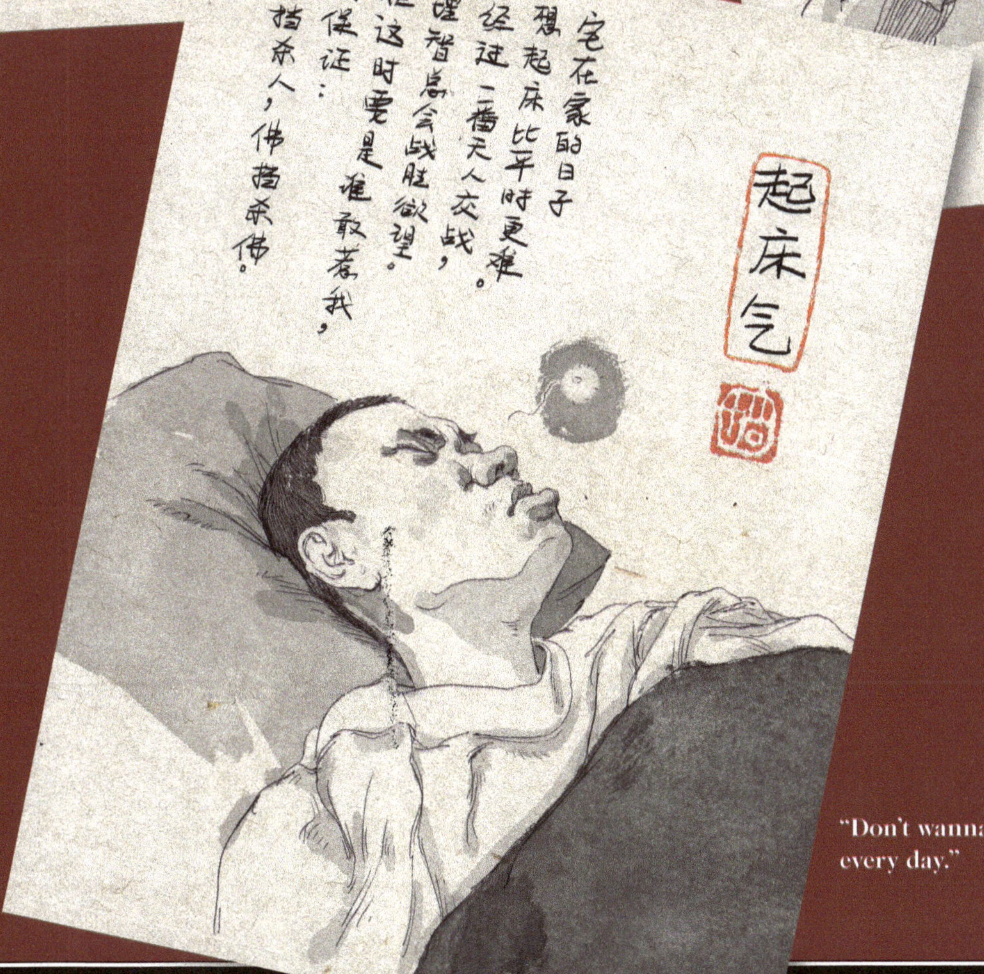
起床气
宅在家的日子
想起床比平时更难
经过一番天人交战，
理智总会战胜欲望。
但这时要是谁敢惹我，
我保证：
人挡杀人，佛挡杀佛。

"Don't wanna get up. The worst moment of every day."

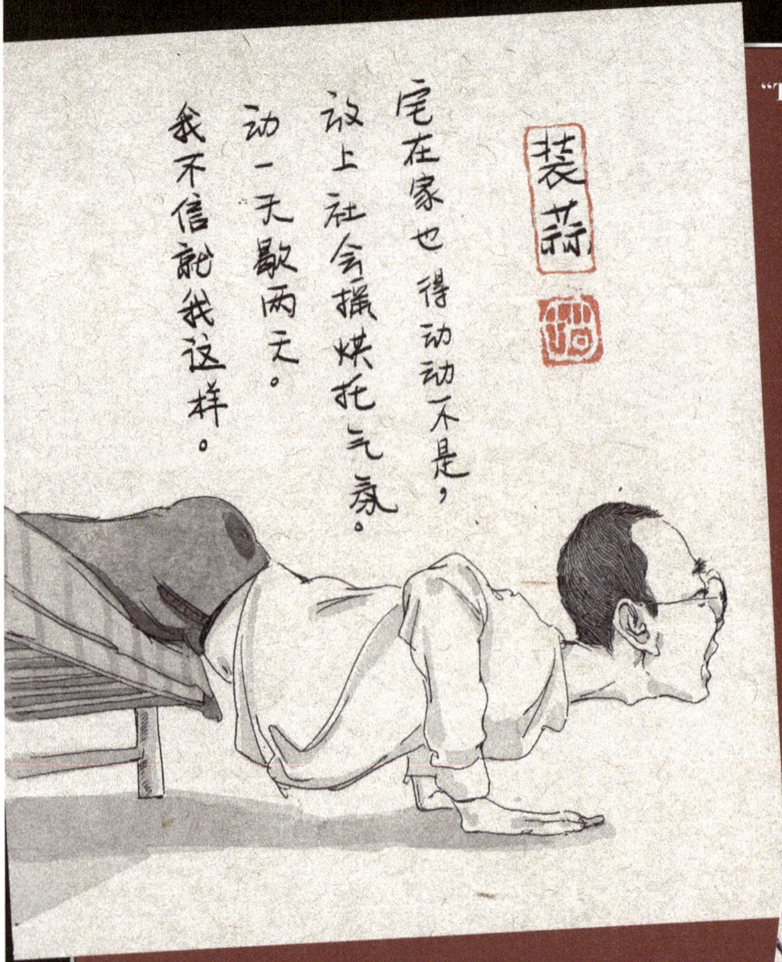
装蒜
宅在家也得动动不是，
赶上社会振烘托气氛。
动一天歇两天。
我不信就我这样。

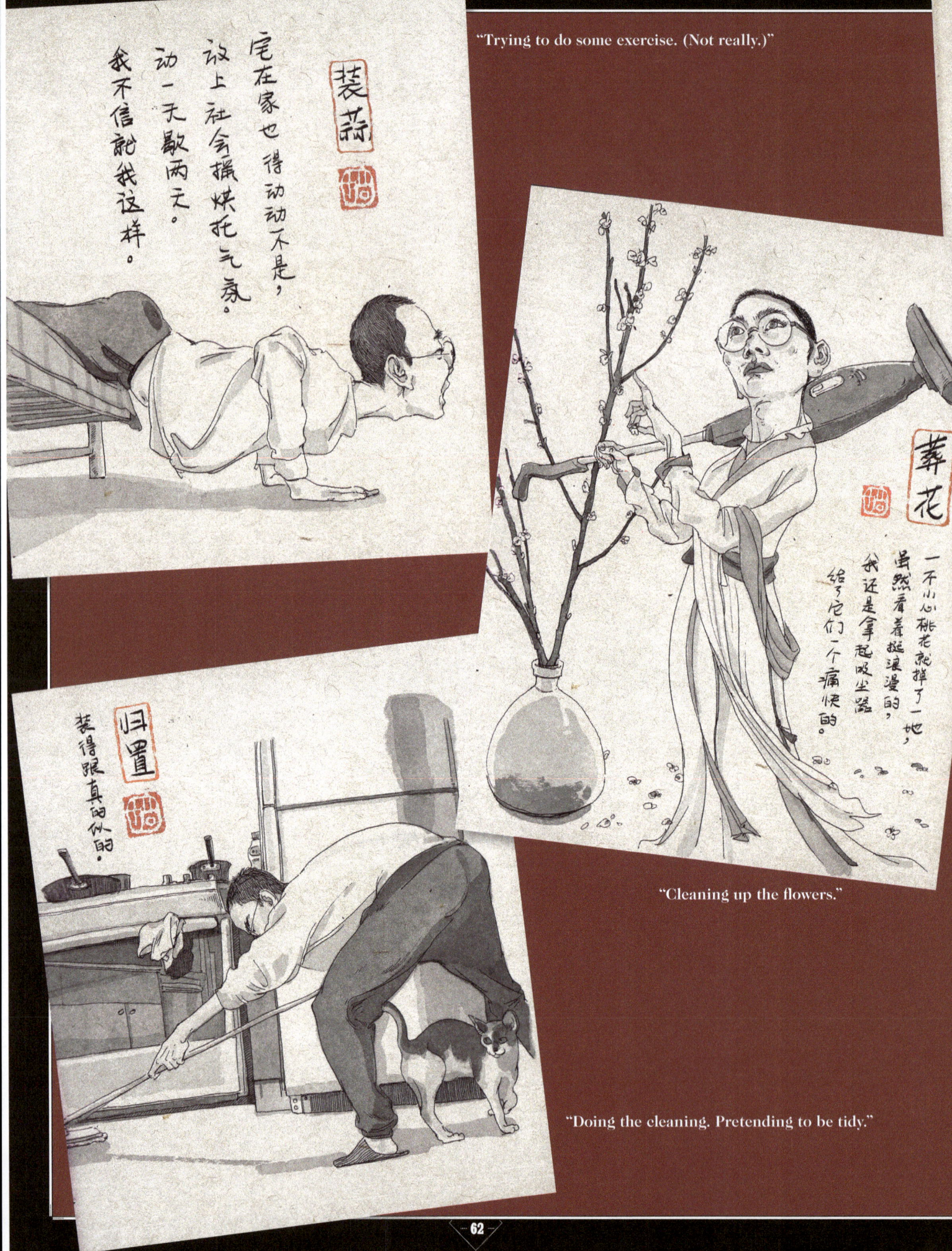

"Trying to do some exercise. (Not really.)"

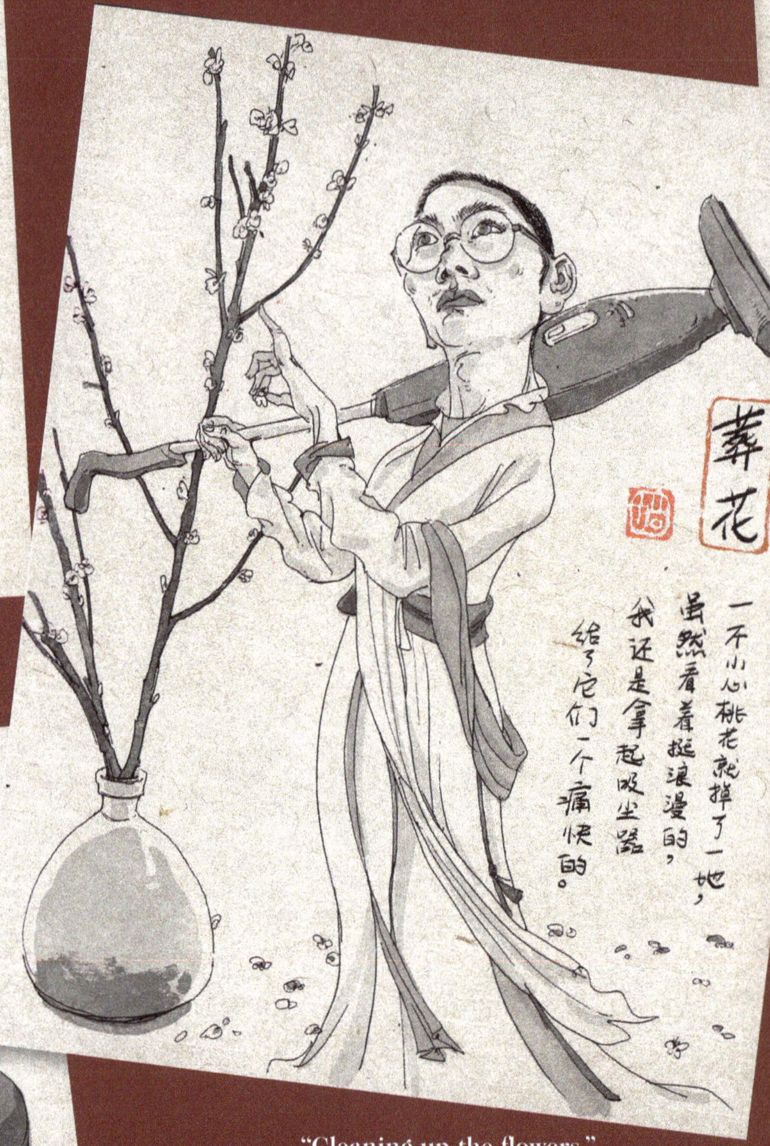
葬花
一不小心桃花就掉了一地，
虽然看着挺浪漫的，
我还是拿起吸尘器
给了它们一个痛快的。

"Cleaning up the flowers."

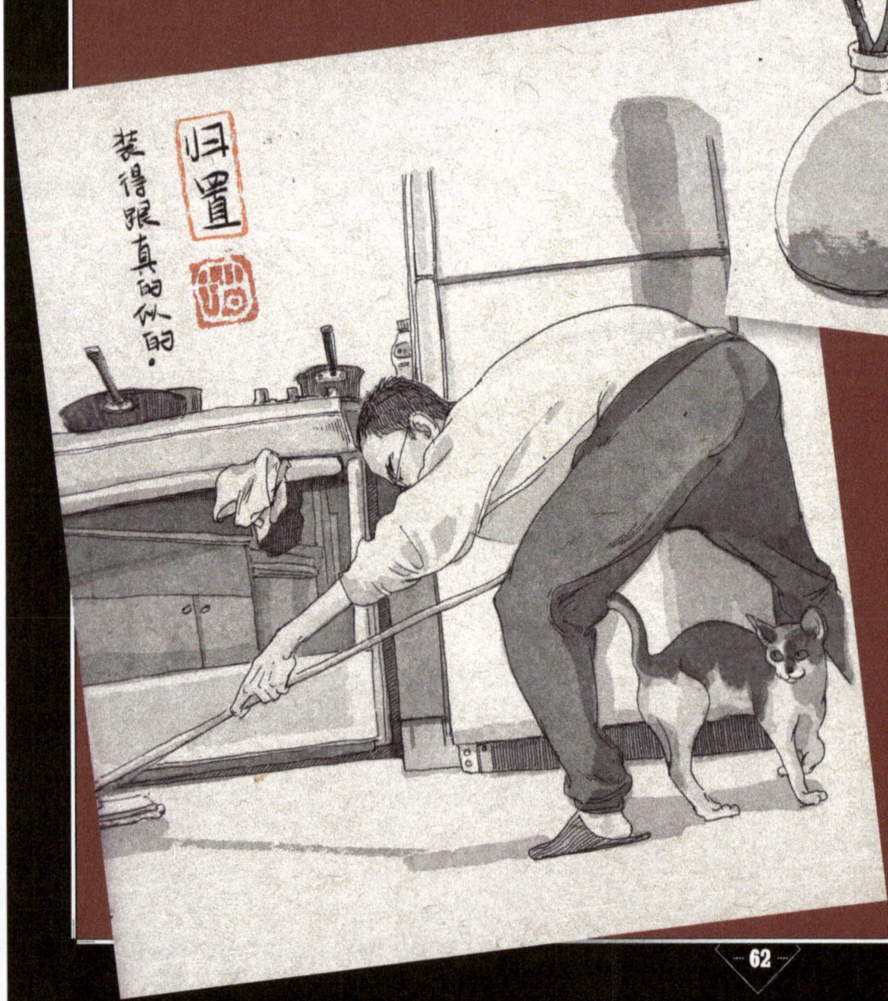
归置
装得跟真的似的。

"Doing the cleaning. Pretending to be tidy."

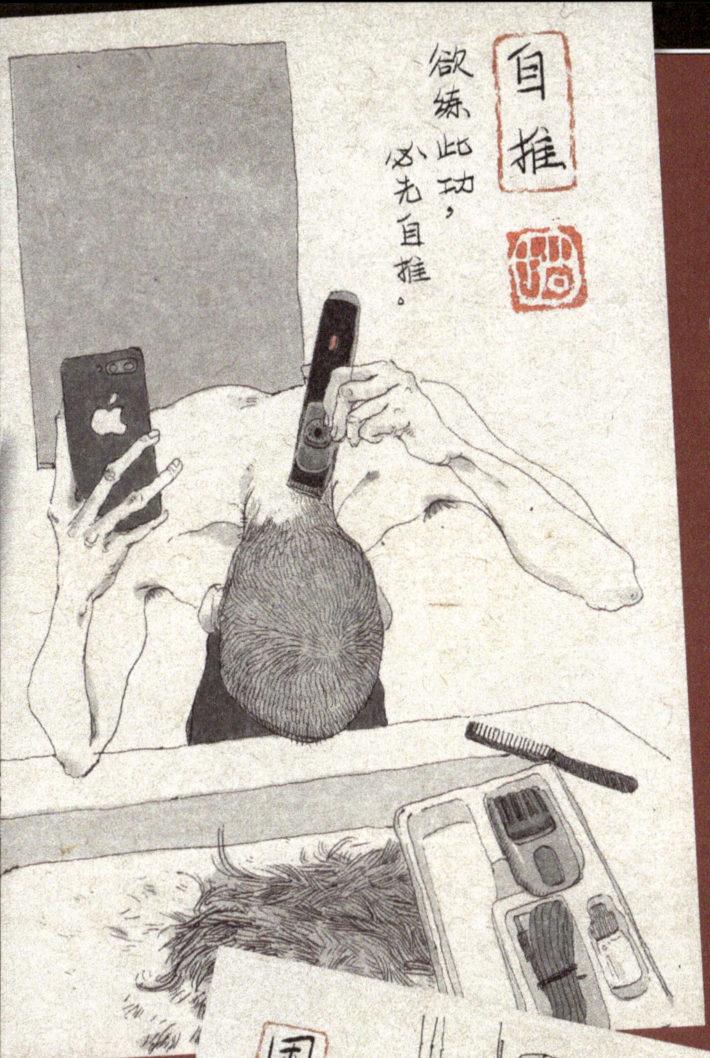
自推
欲练此功，
必先自推。

"Shaving myself. Discovered a new career!"

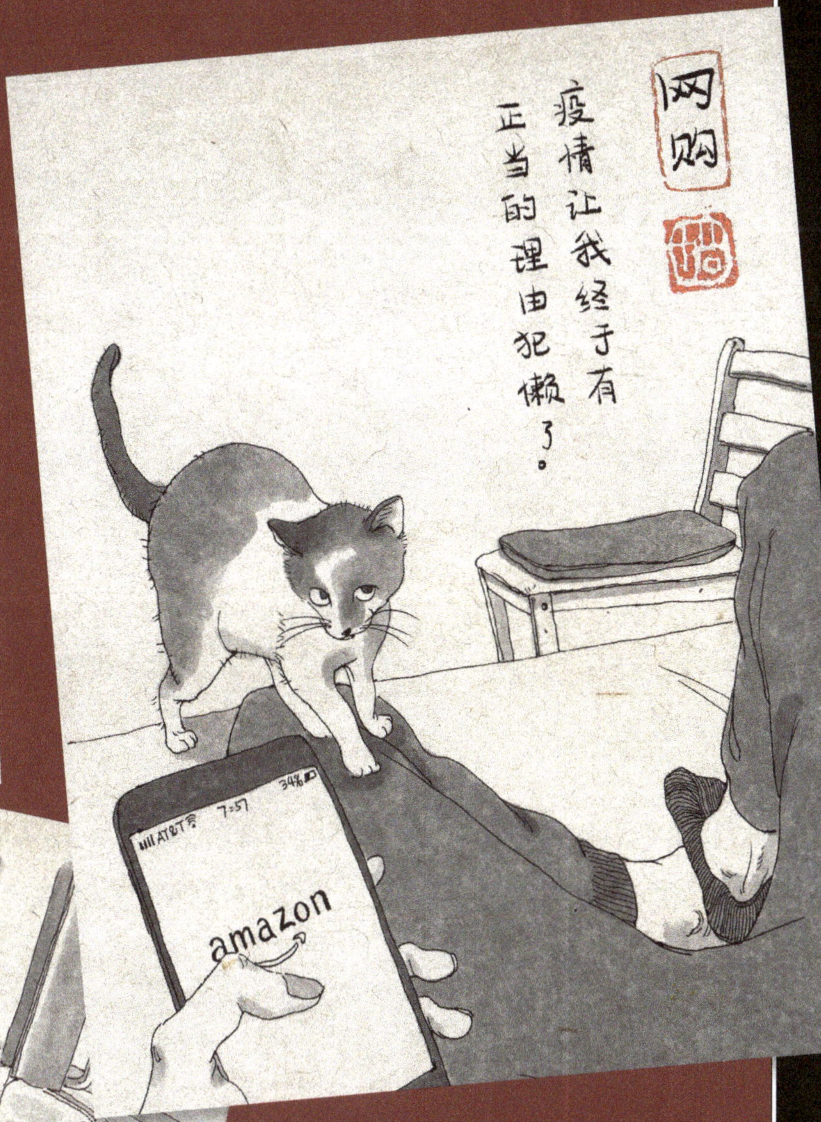
网购
疫情让我终于有
正当的理由犯懒了。
amazon

"Shopping online. Finally got a reason to be lazy."

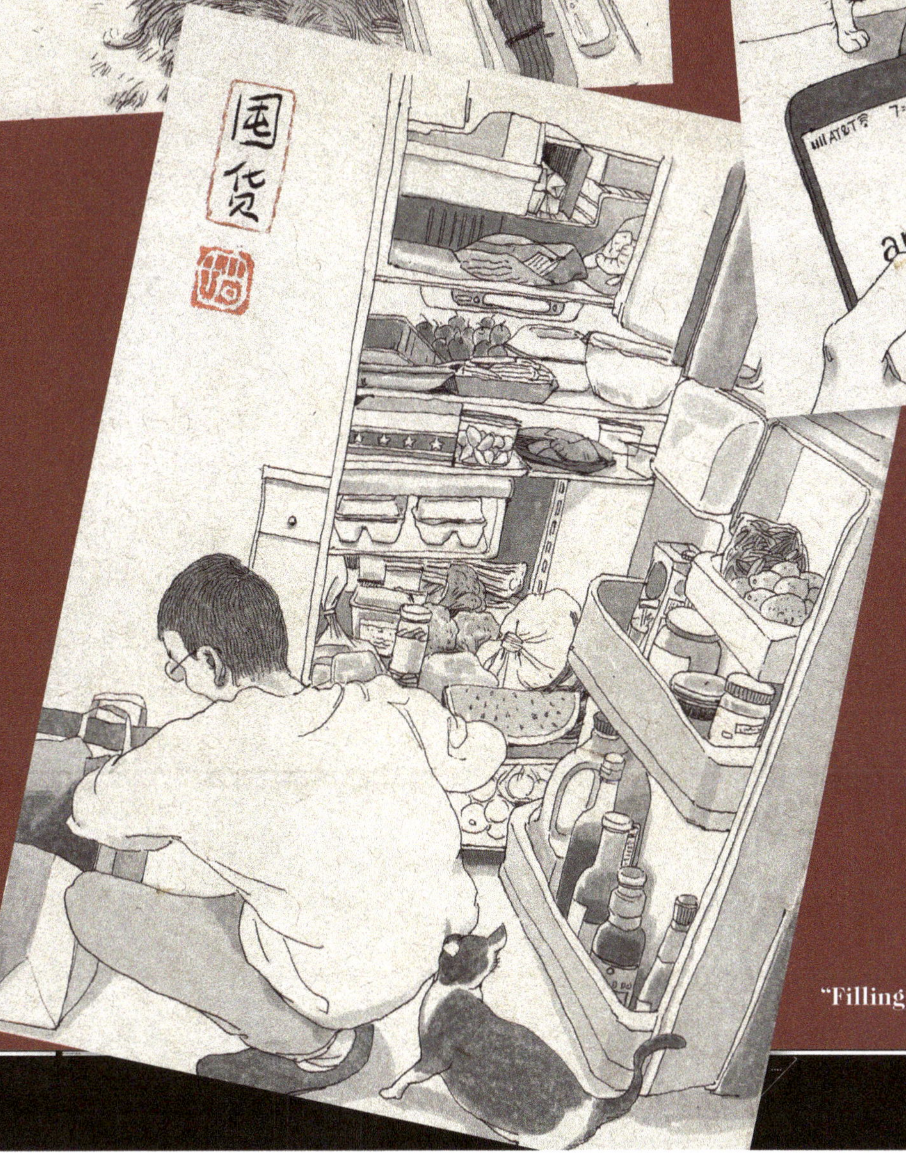
囤货

"Filling up the fridge."

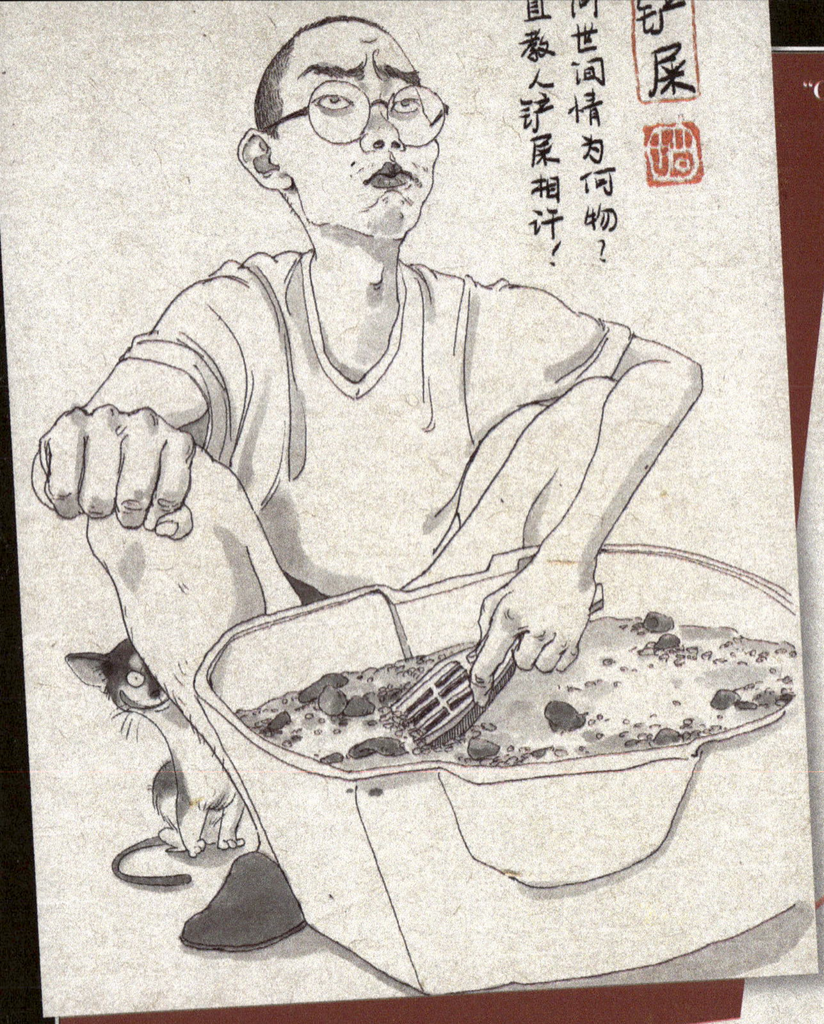

铲屎
问世间情为何物？
直教人铲屎相许！

"Cleaning Timo's litterbox. Literally wanna kill him."

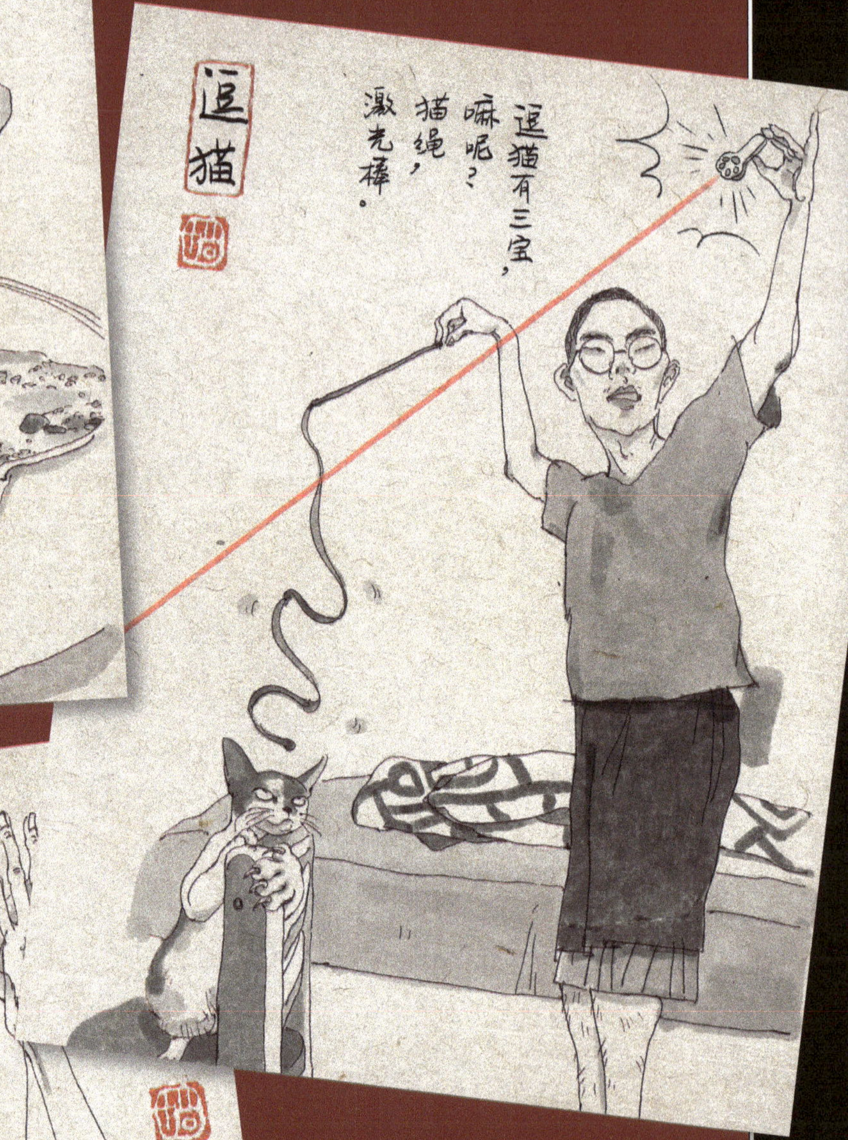

逗猫
逗猫有三宝，
嘛呢？
猫绳，
激光棒。

"Playing with the cat. Timo never notices the laser beam."

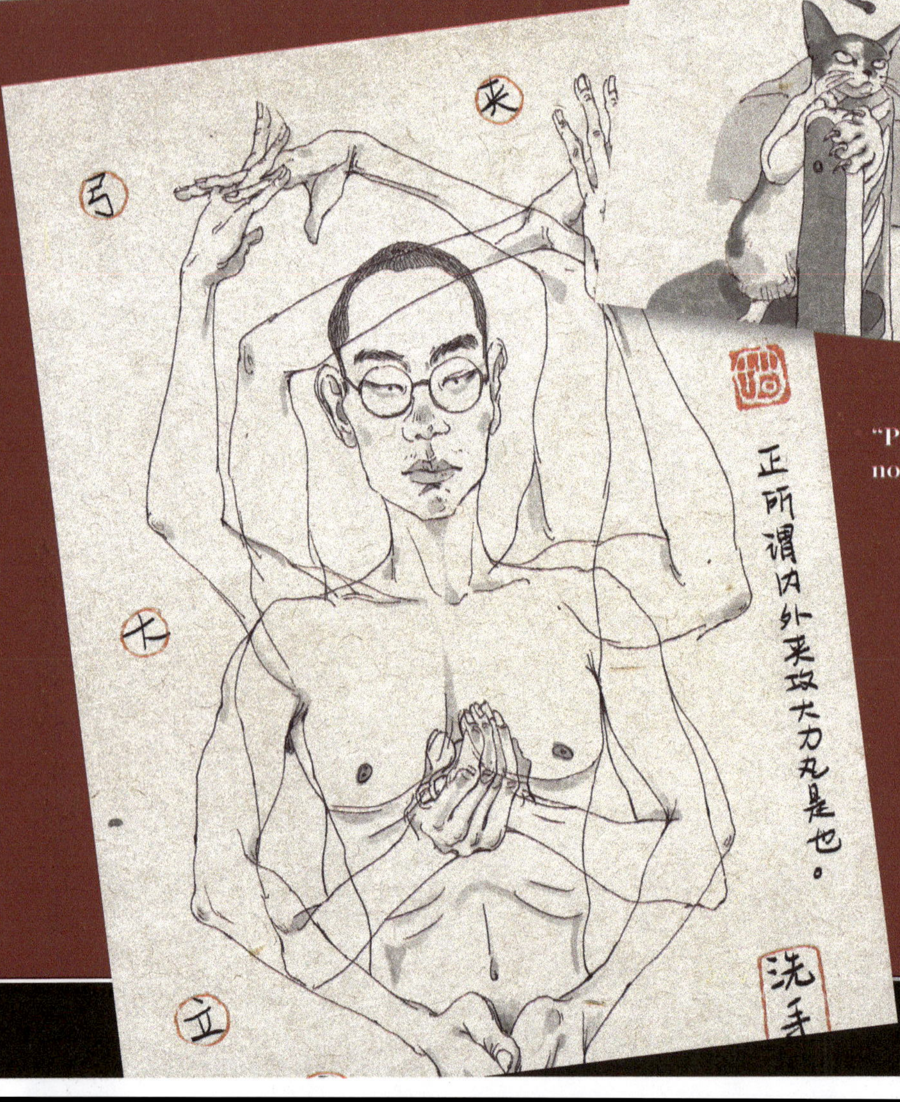

来
弓
下
立
正所谓内外来攻大力丸是也。
洗手

"Hand-washing kung fu."

I was quarantined twice during my childhood: once for the chickenpox in 1968, and again the following year for the Hong Kong flu, which damn near killed me. I almost became one of those half-sized corpses laid out in their Sunday best (as seen in my grandmother's photo album). Around that same time, a friend of mine was quarantined with quinsy, a hideous disease which caused his neck to swell to the circumference of his head. That's what he told me, anyway; he was quarantined and no one could visit. I suppose he could have taken a selfie with his dad's Polaroid, but he didn't. I was ten years old in 1968. I had a babysitter named Jill, who was fifteen and lived just up the street. Jill and I came down with chickenpox simultaneously (who infected whom was unknown) and in order to spare her siblings, the pediatrician prescribed Jill and I to be quarantined together at my house! That's how I spent two weeks of my tenth year with a........

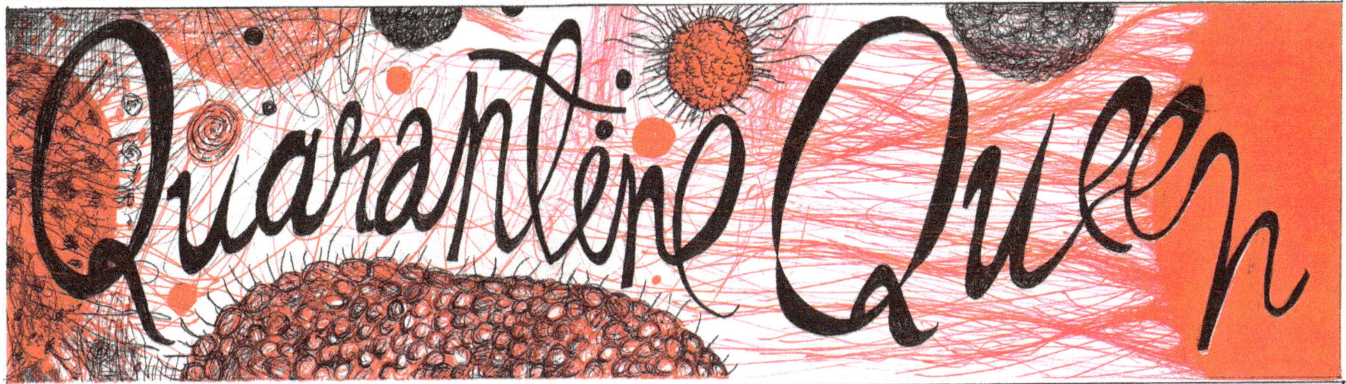
Quarantine Queen

We lived in the beach suburb of Los Angeles known as Playa Del Rey, directly west of LAX. This was a wonderful place to be a kid in the 1960's because a great deal of the land was still nature. We'd take off on our Stingrays to explore the wetlands and estuaries of the southwestern coastal desert, the sand dunes and the cool surf of Dockweiler Beach.

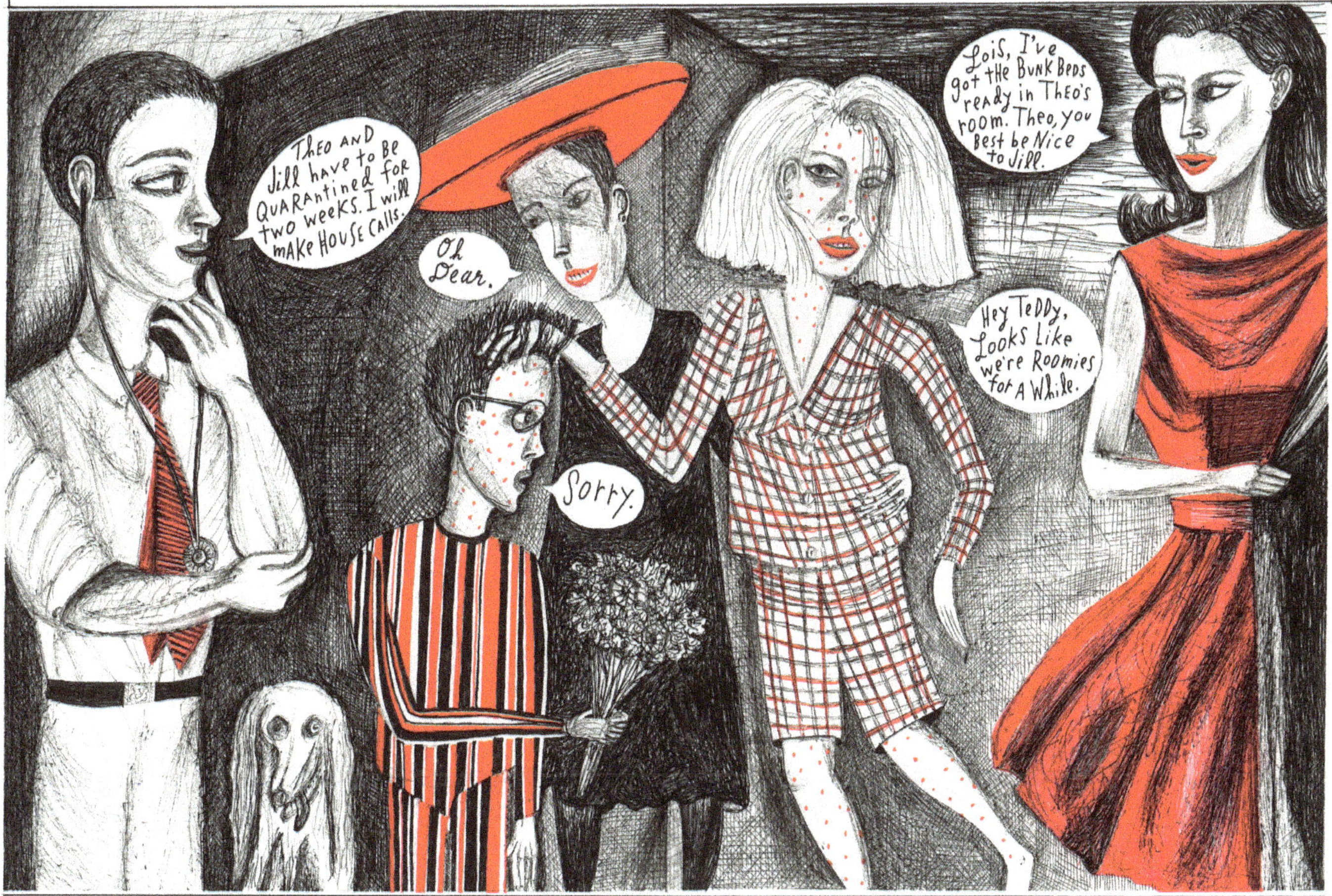
Theo and Jill have to be quarantined for two weeks. I will make house calls.
Oh dear.
Sorry.
Lois, I've got the bunk beds ready in Theo's room. Theo, you best be nice to Jill.
Hey Teddy, looks like we're roomies for a while.

At the age of ten I really didn't need a babysitter, but my father's career required constant travel and my mother worked full time. A highly unusual situation in 1968, but there it was. Jill's dad was a pilot who flew for Western Airlines (something else which no longer exists), and Jill's mom was a housewife with three kids. Jill's dad traveled as much as mine did—sometimes he was the pilot of a flight my dad was on. Our parents were friends and partied on weekends. This was how Jill became my babysitter and my friend.

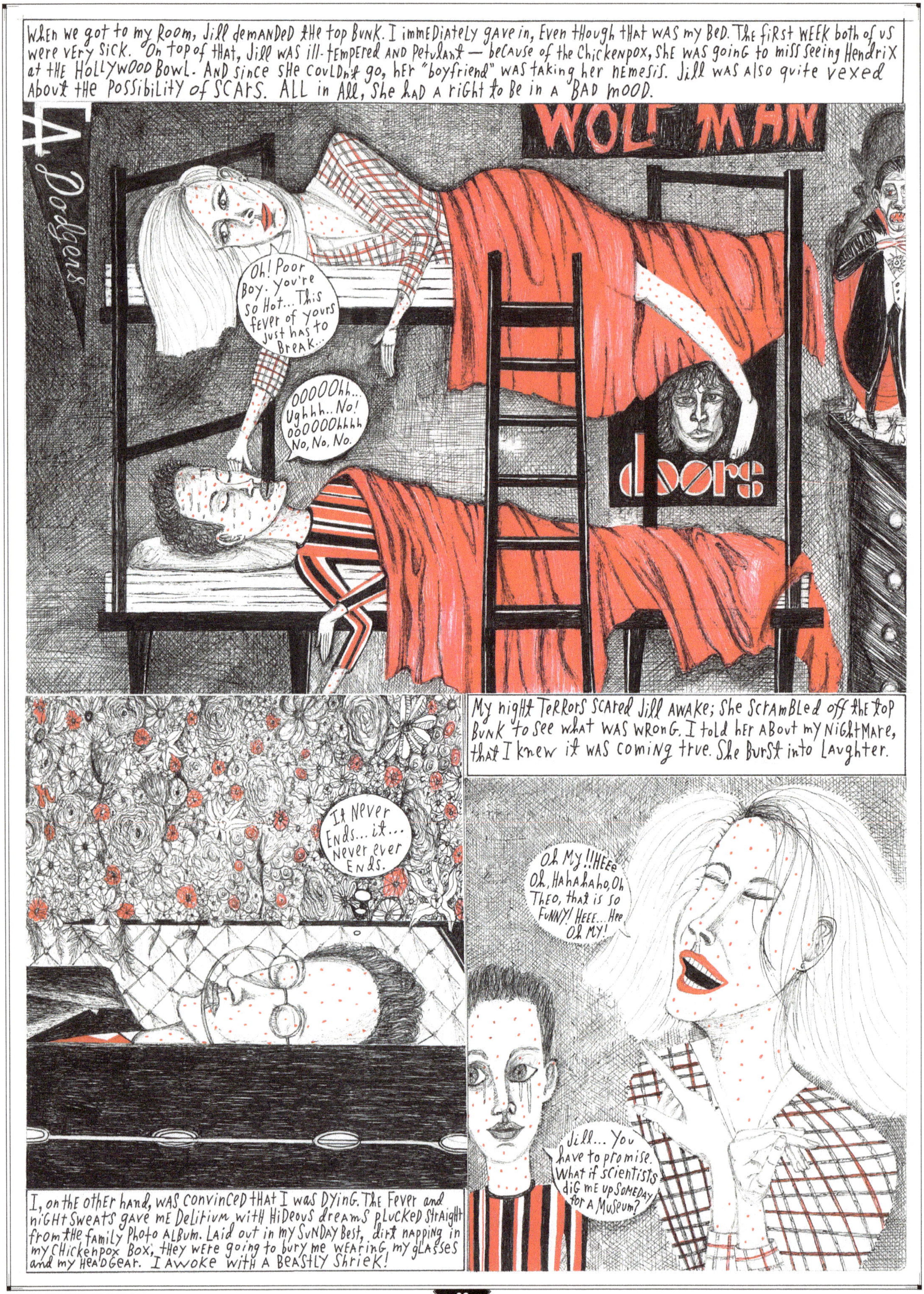
When we got to my room, Jill demanded the top bunk. I immediately gave in, even though that was my bed. The first week both of us were very sick. On top of that, Jill was ill-tempered and petulant — because of the chickenpox, she was going to miss seeing Hendrix at the Hollywood Bowl. And since she couldn't go, her "boyfriend" was taking her nemesis. Jill was also quite vexed about the possibility of scars. All in all, she had a right to be in a bad mood.
LA Dodgers
WOLF MAN
Oh! Poor boy. You're so hot... This fever of yours just has to break...
Ooooohh... Ughhh.. No! Oooooohhhh No, No, No.
doors
My night terrors scared Jill awake; she scrambled off the top bunk to see what was wrong. I told her about my nightmare, that I knew it was coming true. She burst into laughter.
It never ends... it... never ever ends.
I, on the other hand, was convinced that I was dying. The fever and night sweats gave me delirium with hideous dreams plucked straight from the family photo album. Laid out in my Sunday best, dirt napping in my chickenpox box, they were going to bury me wearing my glasses and my headgear. I awoke with a beastly shriek!
Oh my!! Heee Oh, Hahahaho, Oh Theo, that is so funny! Heee... Hee Oh my!
Jill... You have to promise. What if scientists dig me up someday for a museum?

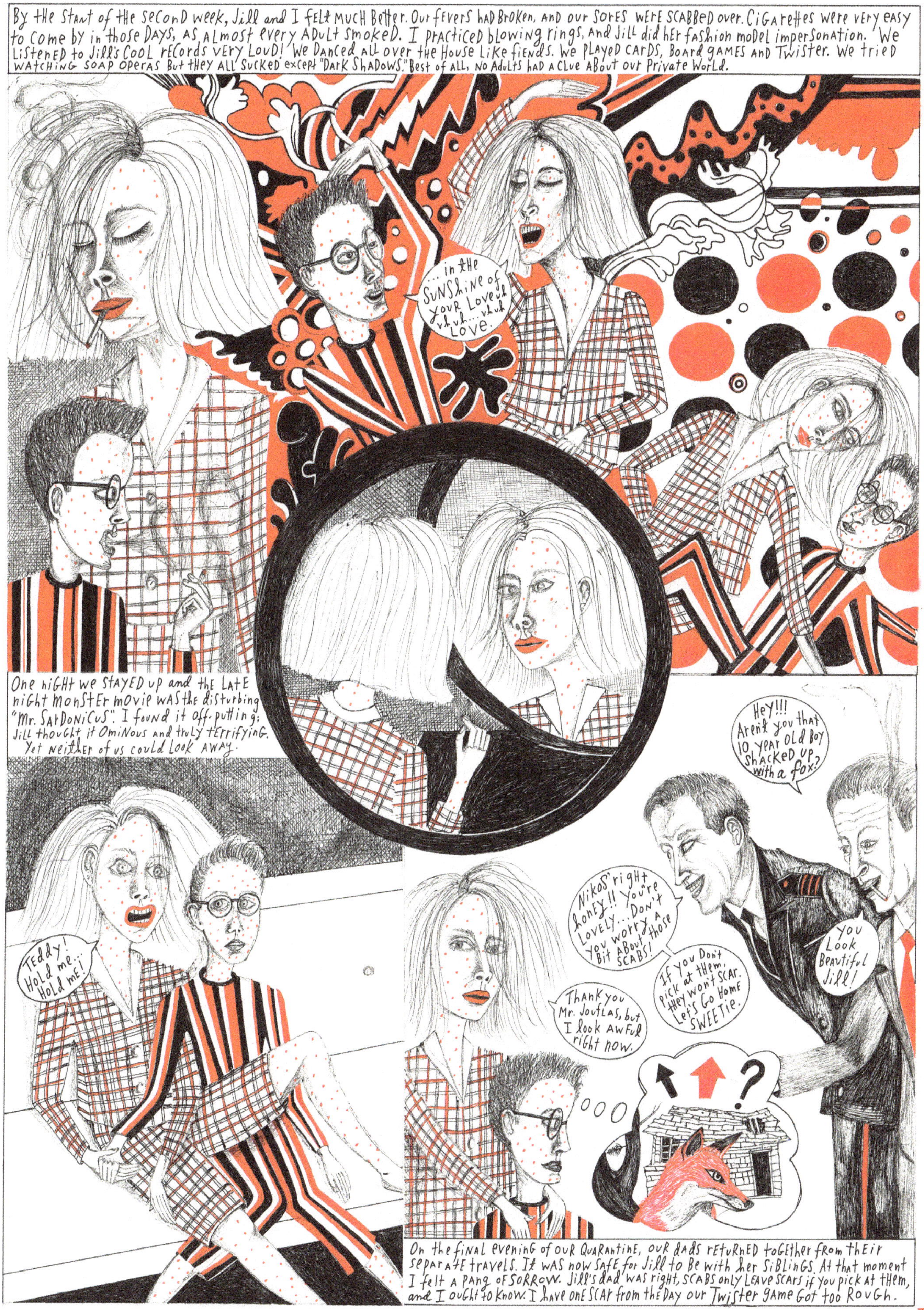
By the start of the second week, Jill and I felt much better. Our fevers had broken, and our sores were scabbed over. Cigarettes were very easy to come by in those days, as almost every adult smoked. I practiced blowing rings, and Jill did her fashion model impersonation. We listened to Jill's cool records very loud! We danced all over the house like fiends. We played cards, board games and Twister. We tried watching soap operas but they all sucked except "Dark Shadows." Best of all, no adults had a clue about our private world.
...in the sunshine of your love uh uh uh... uh uh love.
One night we stayed up and the late night monster movie was the disturbing "Mr. Sardonicus". I found it off-putting; Jill thought it ominous and truly terrifying. Yet neither of us could look away.
Teddy! Hold me... Hold me!
Hey!!! Aren't you that 10 year old boy shacked up with a fox?
Nikos' right honey!! You're lovely... Don't you worry a bit about those scabs!
You look beautiful Jill!
If you don't pick at them, they won't scar. Let's go home sweetie.
Thank you Mr. Jouflas, but I look awful right now.
?
On the final evening of our quarantine, our dads returned together from their separate travels. It was now safe for Jill to be with her siblings. At that moment I felt a pang of sorrow. Jill's dad was right, scabs only leave scars if you pick at them, and I ought to know. I have one scar from the day our Twister game got too rough.
B

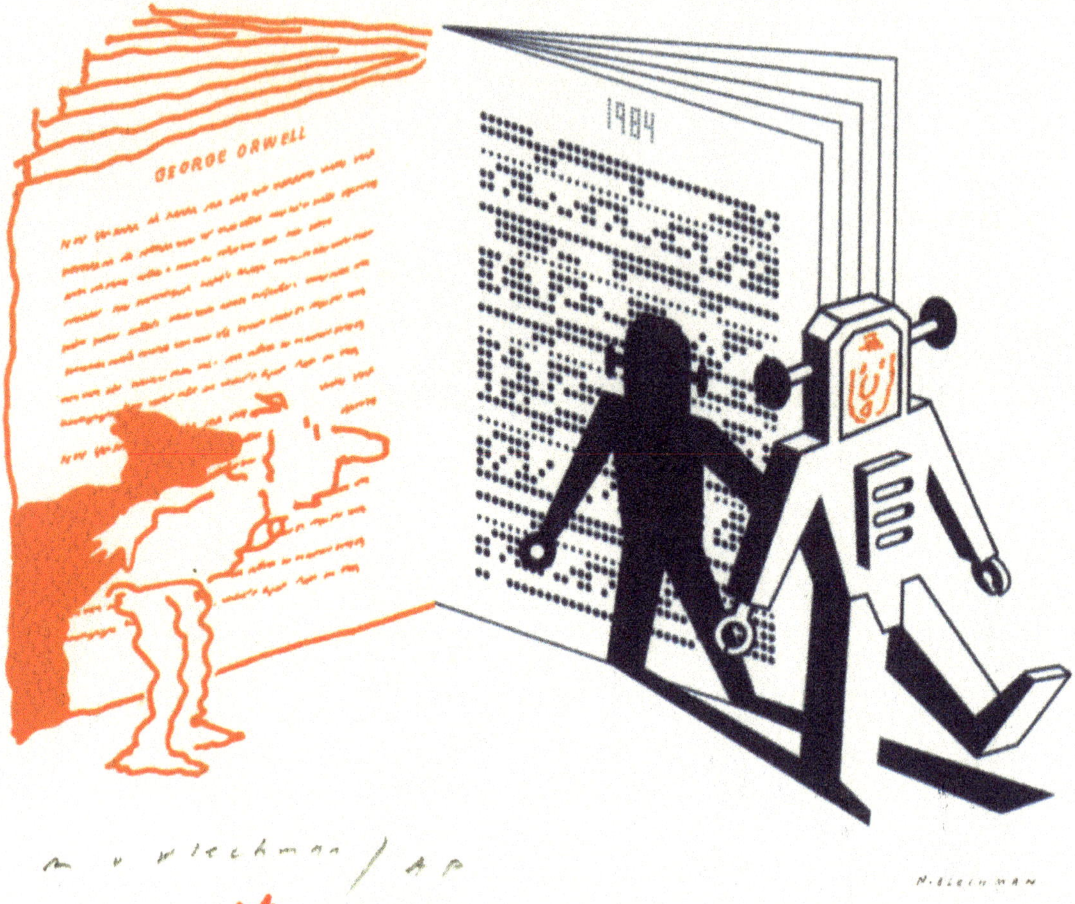
GEORGE ORWELL
1984

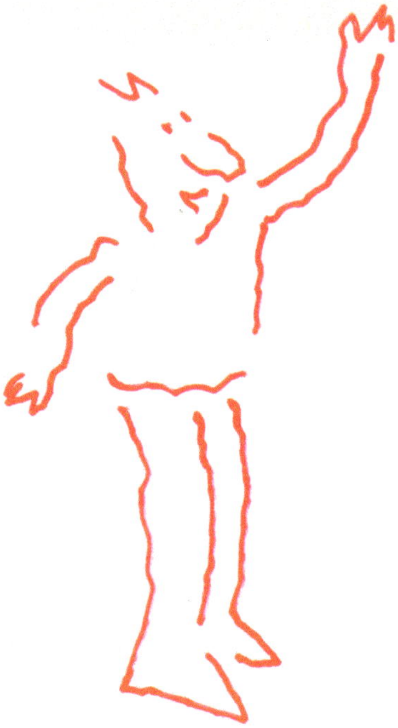

A limited edition of 25 Giclée prints on archival stock, 8" x 10", signed by R. O. Blechman and Nicholas Blechman, is available for $325, postage included. Inquire at ro@roblechman.com.

They'll go fast!

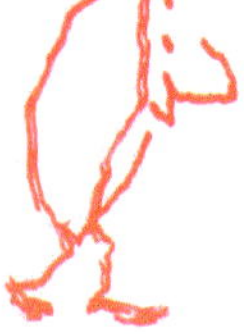

New from ROZ CHAST and PATRICIA MARX

ON SALE NOW

Falling in love is easy. Agreeing about how to load the dishwasher is hard.

You Can Only Yell at Me for One Thing at a Time: Rules for Couples is an illustrated collection of love and romantic advice from *New Yorker* writer Patricia Marx with illustrations by *New Yorker* cartoonist Roz Chast. This is the Valentine's Day and anniversary gift that couples have been waiting for. Available everywhere books are sold.

CeladonBooks.com/bookshop

RALF & BORAX SAY "MAKE HELL YOUR HAPPY PLACE!"

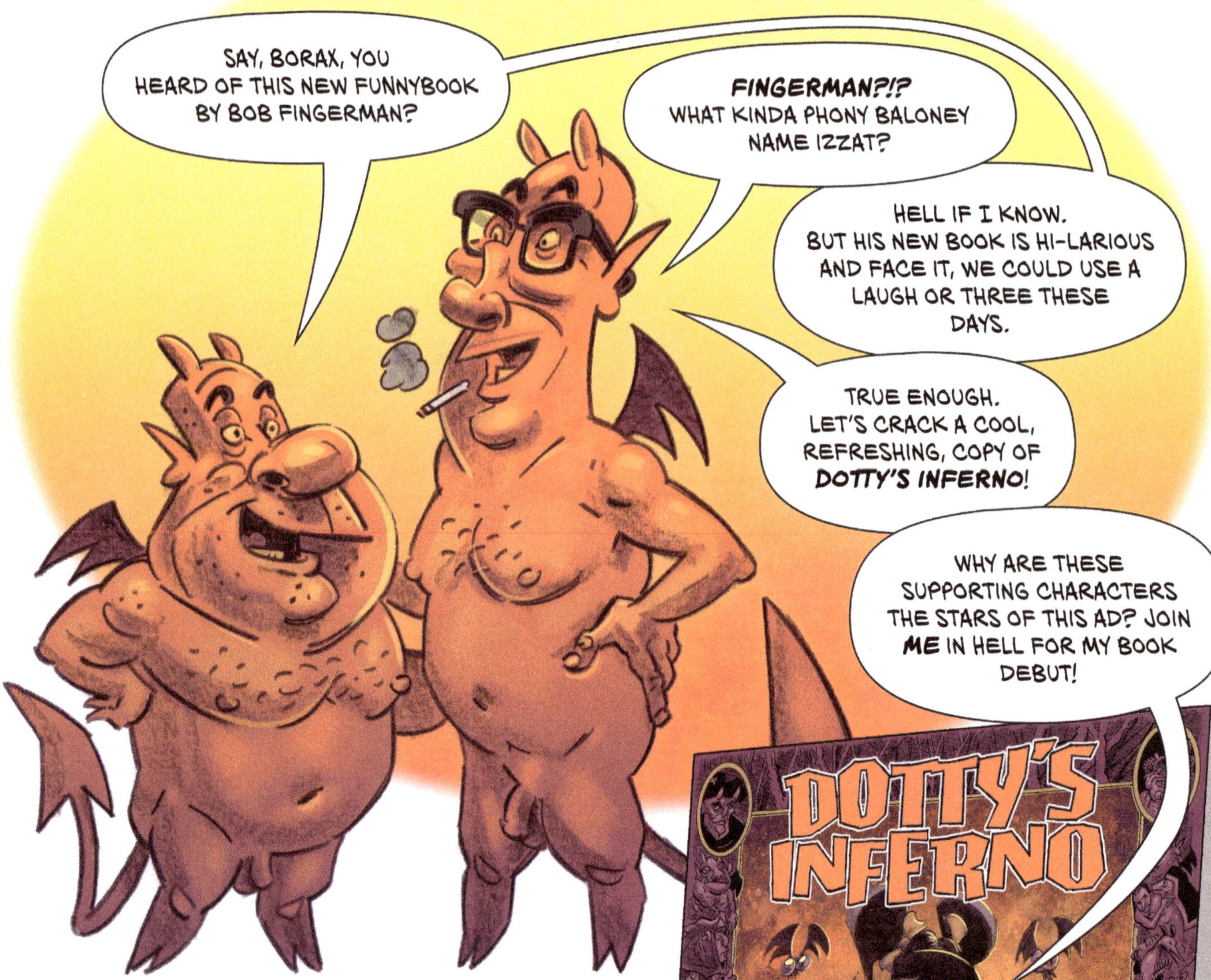
SAY, BORAX, YOU HEARD OF THIS NEW FUNNYBOOK BY BOB FINGERMAN?
FINGERMAN?!? WHAT KINDA PHONY BALONEY NAME IZZAT?
HELL IF I KNOW. BUT HIS NEW BOOK IS HI-LARIOUS AND FACE IT, WE COULD USE A LAUGH OR THREE THESE DAYS.
TRUE ENOUGH. LET'S CRACK A COOL, REFRESHING, COPY OF DOTTY'S INFERNO!
WHY ARE THESE SUPPORTING CHARACTERS THE STARS OF THIS AD? JOIN ME IN HELL FOR MY BOOK DEBUT!

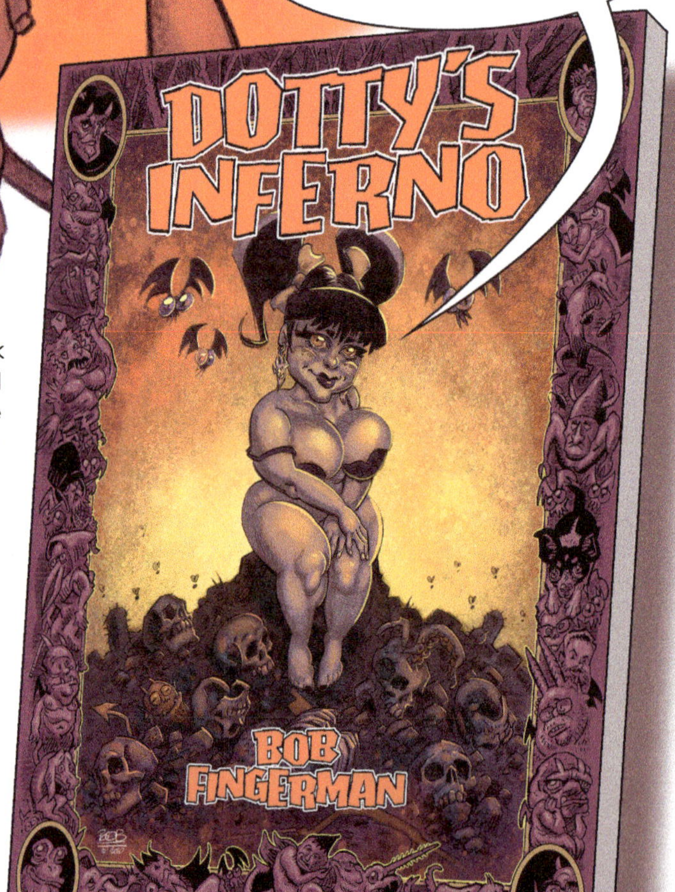
DOTTY'S INFERNO
BOB FINGERMAN

Meet Dotty. In life she was a call girl. In death she's damned to work in Hell's Inhuman Resources department, assigning wayward souls their crummy afterlives. All the same, Dotty spends more time away from her desk on odd jobs and adventures, from fetching Cerberus from Hell's dog pound to licking psychotropic toads' heads and tripping ballz. Forever is a long time, so might as well make the best of a hellish situation.

From the pages of *Heavy Metal* and *Soft Wood*, as well as five never-before-seen stories, ***DOTTY'S INFERNO*** is a roasty romp by *MAD* and *Minimum Wage* cartoonist Bob Fingerman. If Little Annie Fanny and The Checkered Demon had a baby, their hell-spawn might be ***DOTTY'S INFERNO***.

Available for direct orders **NOW!** Get yours from Heavy Metal/ Virus at https://shop.heavymetal.com/collections/virus. In stores in October.

HEAVY METAL VIRUS

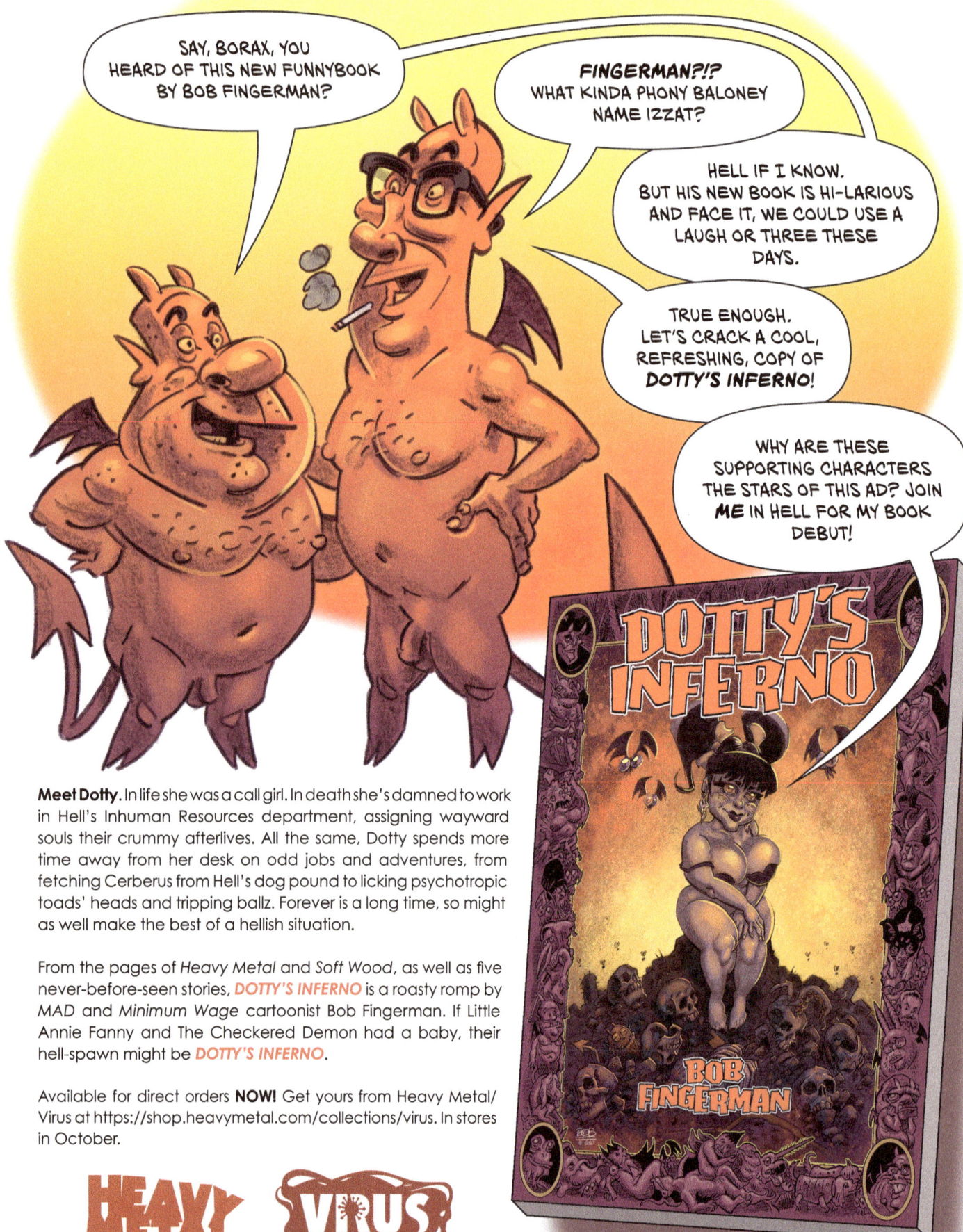

OUR BACK PAGES

NOTES FROM A SMALL PLANET

Hard, but fair • By Rick Geary

MONTHLY WRAP-UP

RICK GEARY © 20

WILL NOT RETURN ITEMS LENT HIM.

NO RAY OF DAY-LIGHT PENETRATES HER SKULL.

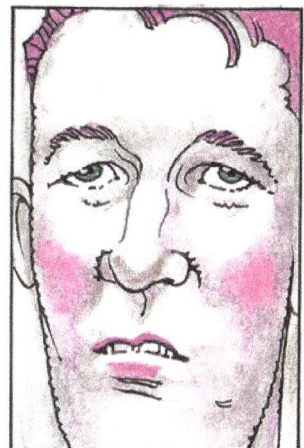
BOASTS OUTRAGEOUSLY OF HIS LOVE CONQUESTS.

HAVE YOU CHECKED OUT HER HAIRBRUSH?

FULL OF "BIG IDEAS" THAT COME TO NOTHING.

TAKES PLEASURE IN TORMENTING HER ADMIRERS.

FAILS TO GRASP THE SIMPLEST OF CONCEPTS.

STUFF BETWEEN HER TEETH.

"KNOWS NOT WHERE HE'S GOING TO."

KEEP IN MIND THAT THESE ARE MY DEAREST FRIENDS AND RELATIONS.

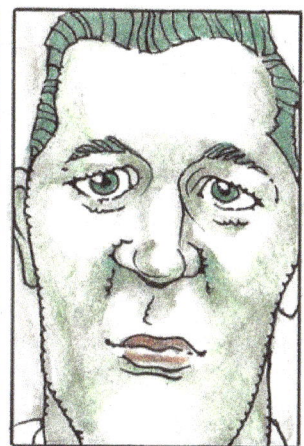
I'M SURE THEY HAVE THEIR ISSUES WITH ME!

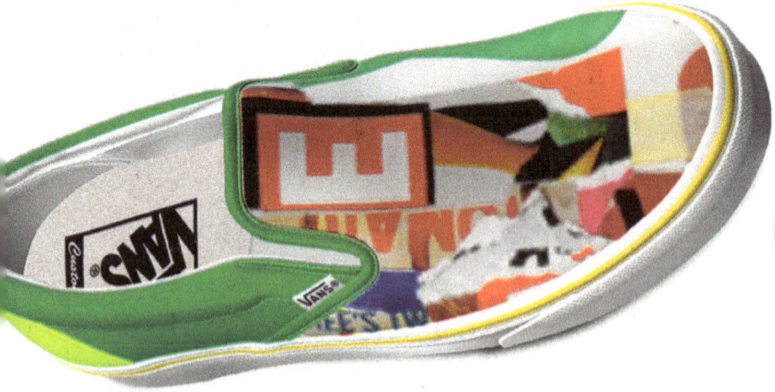

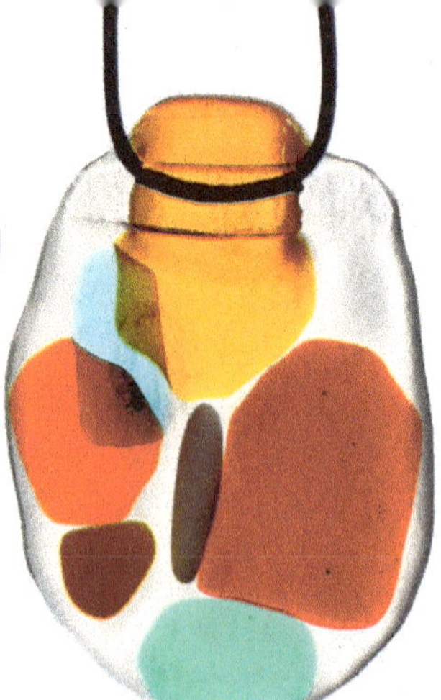

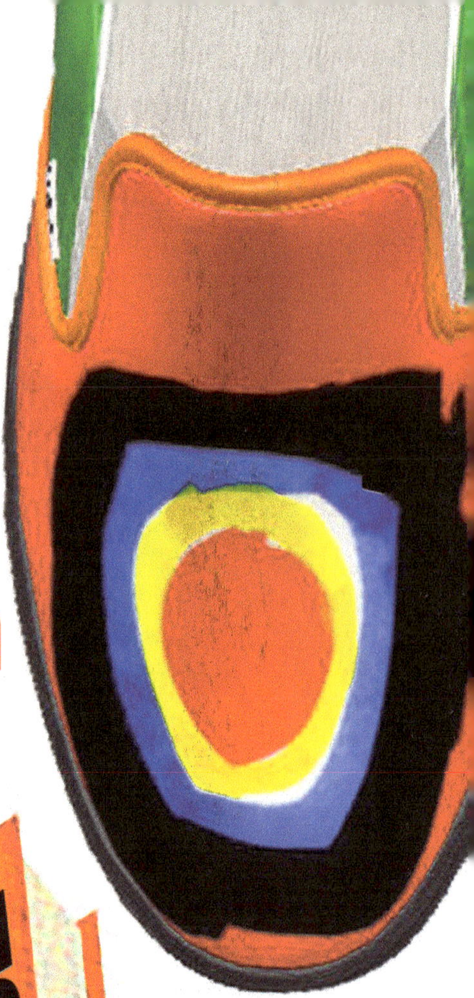

visit www.rosenworld.com

for

Sneakers, Signed Books, Melty Jewels and Original Artwork

by Laurie Rosenwald, First Pancake, Occasional Swede

& America's Favorite Bystander

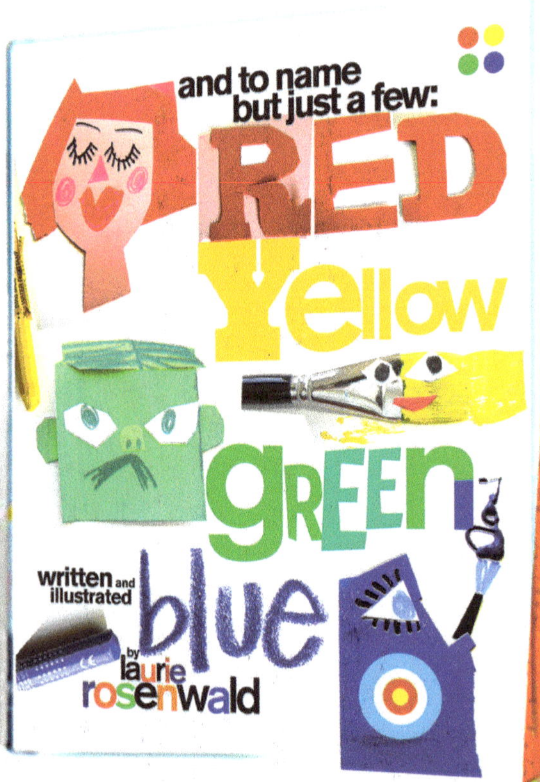
and to name but just a few:
RED
Yellow
gREEn
blue
written and illustrated by laurie rosenwald

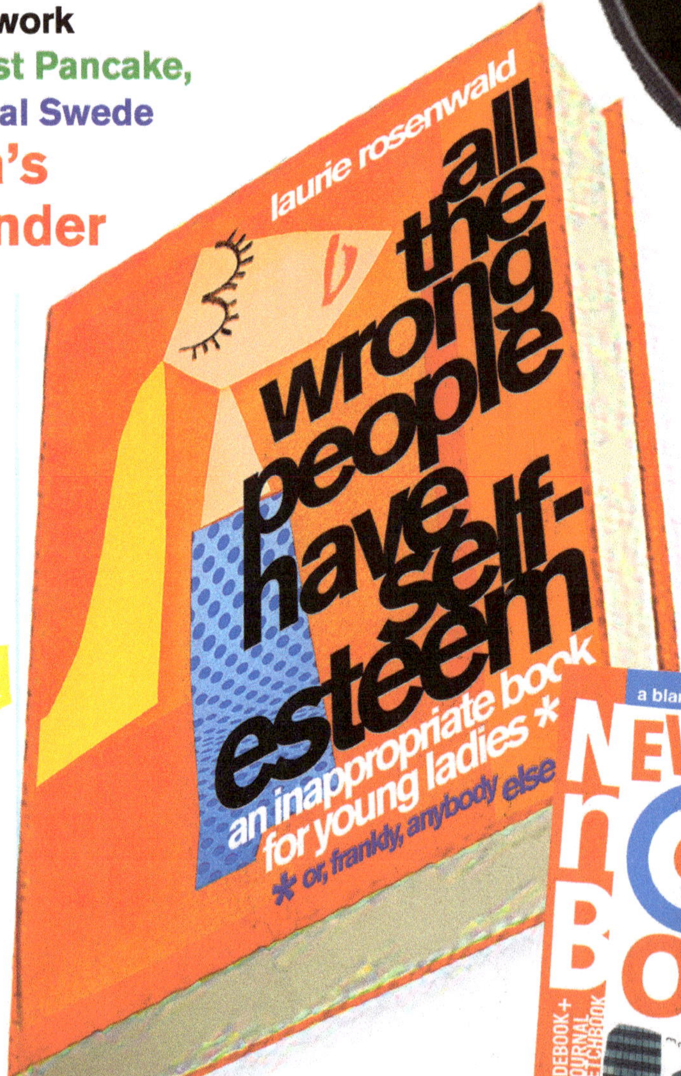
laurie rosenwald
all the wrong people have self-esteem
an inappropriate book for young ladies *
* or, frankly, anybody else

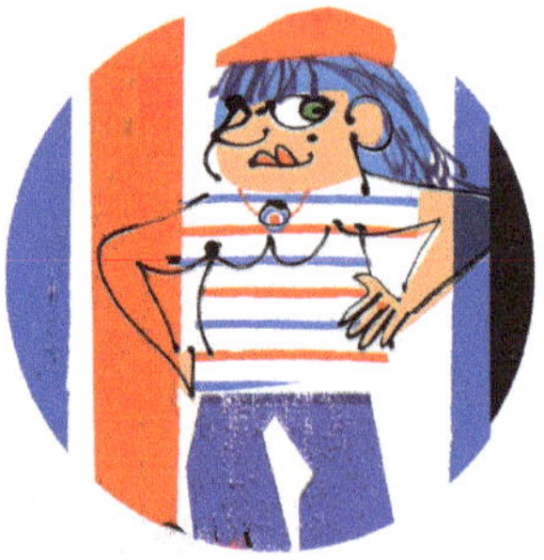

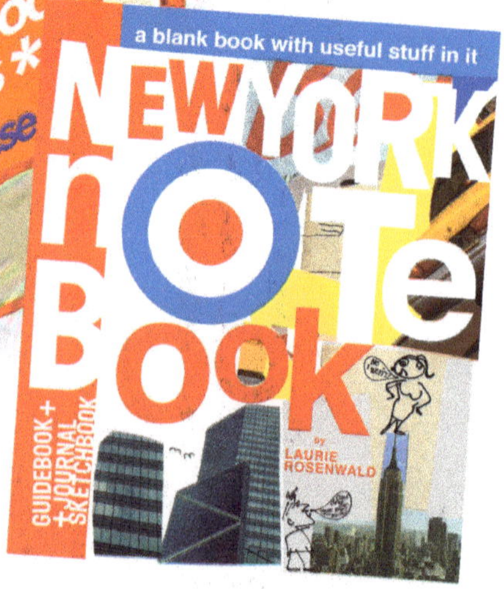
a blank book with useful stuff in it
NEW YORK NOTE BOOK
GUIDEBOOK + JOURNAL + SKETCHBOOK
by LAURIE ROSENWALD

"Laurie's voice is fresh sounding, funny, and completely her own." -David Sedaris

OUR BACK PAGES

WHAT AM I DOING HERE?

Before it was a hot zone, Wuhan was a nice small town… • By Mike Reiss

Woohoo! Wuhan!

When it's not launching plagues, Wuhan is a pretty nice place. With a population of 8.5 million, it's what the Chinese consider "a small town." I was there a few years back as part of a junket, teaching Chinese filmmakers about my work on *The Simpsons*, a show they'd neither watched nor heard of. The lone fan I met had me autograph a Chinese box set of *Simpsons* DVDs that was handsomely packaged and entirely fake. Pretty much everything you buy in China is fake: purses, perfume, pork products. I purchased a fifteen-dollar Rolex in Wuhan that was either a knock-off or selling at a sweet 99.7% discount. "You cannot trust the Chinese," said my Chinese guide, an intense little woman named Yao. "They will screw you over. Big time!"

Yao had conceived and organized this whole trip. Midway through our twelve-hour flight from L.A. to Beijing, she cautioned me that unscrupulous Chinese producers would want to make deals with me. "I will protect you," she said.

"Thank you."

"I want five percent!" She pulled a contract from her (fake) Louis Vuitton handbag. I signed the document, fearing that if I didn't, she would push me off the plane at 30,000 feet. I hadn't even landed in China and I'd already been extorted. Yao didn't seem happy either. As the jet touched down in Beijing, she told me, "Five percent is too low. I want ten!"

"No! I already signed a contract. *Your* contract!"

She moaned. Being Chinese, Yao had even screwed over Yao.

First stop in Beijing was with the Chinese Minister of Animation. "I regulate every cartoon produced in China and report on each studio to the government," explained this unsmiling man in an old-school woolen Mao jacket. "I am also the voice of Chinese Donald Duck."

The Minister showed me his newest project: Peking Opera stories adapted to cartoon form. He hoped these would get teenagers interested in this ancient Chinese art. He showed me one five-minute cartoon, and asked my opinion. "You must be honest," he said, taking a grim pull from a coffee mug emblazoned with a grinning Donald Duck.

"Honestly? I found it really boring and couldn't imagine a teenager enjoying it."

"I see," he grunted. "We have made one hundred and forty of those."

And this is the problem: the Chinese have the fastest-growing movie business in the world, producing films that gross billions domestically and zilch overseas. Chalk it up to cultural differences: foreigners don't like bad movies. And they are *bad*—ponderous historical dramas, sexless romances, and comedies so screechy and pointless, not even the French enjoy them.

From Beijing, we moved on to Harbin, Hubei, Guangzhou, Guangdong, Gangplow, and Guanaco. They're all cities larger than New York, and I'd never heard of any of them—have you? If so, you're lying—Gangplow is a farming tool and Guanaco is a kind of llama. All these cities are built on the basic Chinese model —plow under three millennia of history and replace it with gleaming clusters of skyscrapers, shopping malls, KFC's and knock-offs of KFC (KLC, KLG, UFO, and yes, "OFC—Obama Fried Chicken").

My favorite city was Guangdong—called Canton when we were kids, it was rechristened Guangdong in the dumbest name change since Kanye West became Yeezy. The city is filled with the kind of weird wonders you'd only see in China:

• The parks are packed with old people playing hacky-sack (actually, a local variant, featuring a dart on a spring). They play it all day long and are really good at it. Why do they do it? The government told them to, to keep them busy. And they'll keep at it till the government gives them permission to stop. Or die.

• The entire skyline—two dozen buildings—have been covered with LEDs, and every night, the city becomes one big video screen. This being China, they have all the technology and no idea what to do with it—the night I was there, the presentation was ten minutes of giant goldfish swimming from building to building. They'd basically turned the whole city into a screensaver.

• They built a long glass observation deck protruding over a thousand-foot deep gorge. To make this even scarier, the dick-shaped deck juts out from the crotch of a giant concrete sculpture of King Kong. Or rather, a rip-off of King Kong—it wouldn't be a Chinese attraction without some copyright infringement. But make no mistake: the King Kong of Guangdong has a long dong.

While in Guangdong, I visited the animation studio that produced Bunko, "the Bart Simpson of China." And their Bart looked a lot like our Bart—spiky hair, blue shorts, yellow skin. The only difference was Bunko was twice as tall. And had no nose. I met Bunko's creator, a handsome young man called "the Matt Groening of China" who had a much bigger, nicer office than Matt Groening, "the Matt Groening of America." Bunko's bunker was a six-story animation complex, with state-of-the-art studios, art gallery, and gift shop. What they didn't have was viewers. Though they assured me Bunko was a world-wide phenomenon, no one I met in China had ever heard of it. Animation fans have

MIKE REISS is Intrepid Traveler for *The American Bystander*.

Explore the world's largest cartoon database

Over **500,000** cartoons from the **Bystander, New Yorker** & more

CARTOONCOLLECTIONS.COM

---

never heard of it. Google has never heard of it. The whole gorgeous studio may have been a front for a meth lab. Maybe that's why they called him Bunko.

Nothing much had come of this junket until I met Dr. Fu (not his real monosyllable), "the Walt Disney of China." By now you may have noticed that everything in their country is "the [BLANK] of China." Their top attraction should be called "'The Great Wall of China' of China."

Dr. Fu owns China's largest amusement park; he also runs the best aquarium I've ever visited and the only entertaining circus I've ever seen. (Screw you, Cirque du Soleil.) And he owns a zoo packed to the rafters with exotic animals. Think rhinos an endangered species? Not at Fu Zoo, where you see way too many rhinos, all packed into one enclosure. Excited to see one panda cub? This zoo has the world's only set of panda triplets, in clear violation of China's one-child policy. Are they really triplets? All panda cubs look alike, so it's possible they grabbed three cubs from three mothers and put them in one pen. Or that they pumped one poor panda mom full of fertility drugs. Or they fattened up and repainted some beagle puppies. My theory is that Dr. Fu put a gun to a female panda's head and hissed in her ear, "Have triplets." For Dr. Fu is a very intimidating character, so much so that I'm going to call him Dr. Wo for the rest of this article. Even his alias needs an alias.

Wo gets what Wo wants, and on this visit Wo wanted *me*. He invited me to his private dining room, where, in true Bond villain fashion, one entire wall was a tank of great white sharks. "I want you to make an animated film about my panda triplets. And fifty-two episodes of a panda cartoon series," he told me. "How long will that take?"

It would probably take four years, but knowing he wouldn't have the patience for that, I told him two years.

"I want it in six months," he said.

"You got it!" I told him. It was a physically impossible task, but no one says no to Wo. As his assistant lamented to me, "He once ordered me to get him a whale. Where do you buy a whale?"

My tour guide Yao emailed me that night, warning me to be careful dealing with Dr. Wo. "I know," I wrote back, "he's a slippery character."

And, for reasons I'll never figure out, Yao forwarded my email to Dr. Wo. The man had just made me a hugely generous offer and I called him a slippery character. Wo canceled our deal, and Yao and I returned to America empty-handed.

Why did she do it? This could be a million-dollar deal. With the 5% commission she extorted from me, Yao stood to clear a cool fifty thousand dollars. It's like she knew that in a Chinese deal, *someone* had to get screwed—even if it meant double-crossing her own client, and as a result, herself.

Since that visit to China, Yao and I haven't spoken. One of the local mayors I met has gone to jail. Dr. Wo has been accused of flying helicopters at night into Africa to kidnap giraffes. No one has ever seen a Bunko cartoon. And I learned that every night at midnight in Times Square, all the buildings light up in an elaborate video show even better than the one in Guangzhou.

It's just three blocks from my apartment. But who wants to go to Times Square at midnight?

P.S. MUELLER THINKS LIKE THIS

The cartoonist/broadcaster/writer is always walking around, looking at stuff • **By P.S. Mueller**

The Blight Stuff

In July of 2026 some self-styled bio-hacker kid released a modified spore into the North Dakota wind, and within three years most of the world's crops lay all dark and soupy in the fields. The kid was no doubt just another angry farm punk bent on messing with Big Ag and his identity remains unknown, but we do know it had to be a kid. (It's always a kid, like that "Zak 345" who brought down the Zion nuclear reactor with concrete weevils in 2019.) Also, there is no way any professional bioengineer would sabotage work that successfully overfed everyone to the point where hip replacements ranked first among graduation presents. Those were the days.

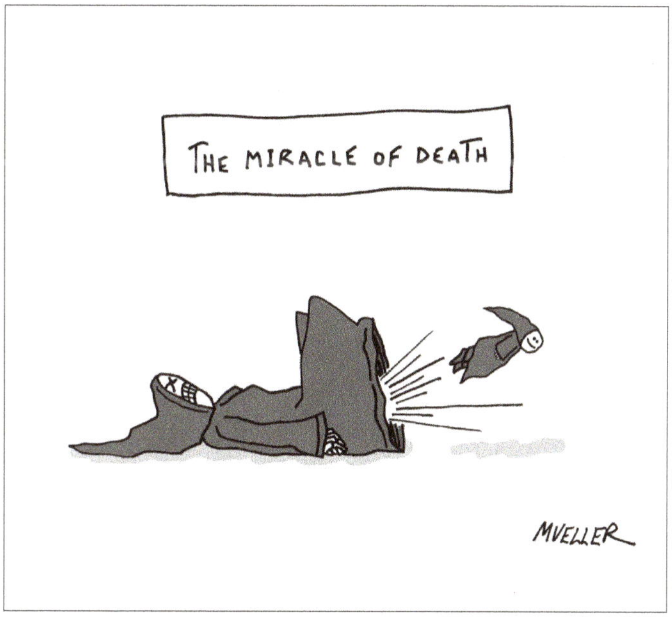
THE MIRACLE OF DEATH
MUELLER

I happened to be in the artificial animal protein game at the time, running a startup with my brother Hal. We had figured out a way to grow Angus beef muscle in a variety of popular shapes and were on our way to huge returns with our patented line of pleated ribeyes. We named our company Beeeft, mainly because some kid in IT said it would look cool on the internet. But the crop failures caught Hal and me and every other tissue-bather in the business totally flat-footed. Overnight, even oil companies wanted to invest in us. Capital poured in and millions of gallons of liquid nutrients flooded out over square mile muscle-sucking vats of ChickyShapes, Pigtail Valley Ham Slabs, and Lambfoolery. (Veal eluded us—it's hard to impose cruelty on a small lump in a warm puddle.)

We worked like those things that used to bark. The world had no choice but to change rapidly to a 100% animal protein diet or perish. Green energy, coal, nuclear, natural gas and oil were all diverted to the production of the cheapest and most quickly harvested form of a rather salty cured product dubbed "Balono." Soon, those who survived came to subsist almost exclusively on Balono. Attempts to use petroleum-based substrates to fashion something approximating rye bread have not gone well, though interesting research into leavened clam gel shows promise and may be available next week once the FDA signs off on it.

The vast majority of the world's consumers bravely adapted to Balono and went on with the task of making more of it, especially now that the only remaining employment for most was at least peripherally directed toward that effort. Of course, in rural pockets here and there, a wild-eyed race of heirloom farmers emerged, their crops guarded jealously with armaments acquired from gun fetishists in return for a few golden potatoes and a handful of chives. This tribe steadily retreated to the north and disappeared entirely from mailing lists early last year.

It took a decade, but an eventual recovery to a somewhat more diversified economy began to take shape. Bankers returned to their long-abandoned roosts to trade in Balono futures; real estate soon followed. But before long a growing disenchantment with Balono forced the animal protein industry to diversify as well. People wanted choice, new flavor enhancers, something less greasy and fattening—a little treat to go along with that Lipitor sundae with Aspartame sprinkles after church.

And so, today, with the help of a massive government loan, Hal and I are announcing the first in a series of tests aimed at creating artificial carrots from the DNA of rabbits.

"You Will Never Be Alone"

—Comfort and fear in one sentence.

You have a 100% chance of being eaten by a bear.

I am the new bear in town. I can read and write and talk. I got hungry while I was nosing around the dumpster, see? I wrote this note and handed it to you.

I'm going to eat you and shit you out behind a tree. I could have just as easily roared and snapped you like a twig, but I'm not that kind of bear. I'm a vampire bear. B

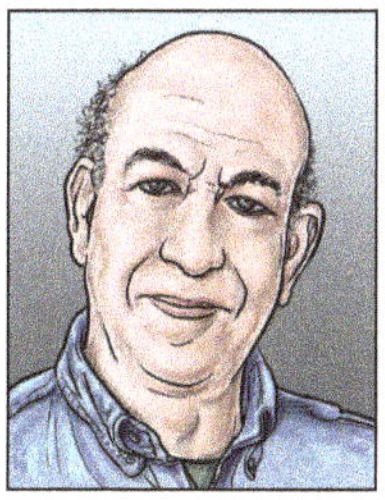

P.S. MUELLER is Staff Liar of *The American Bystander*.

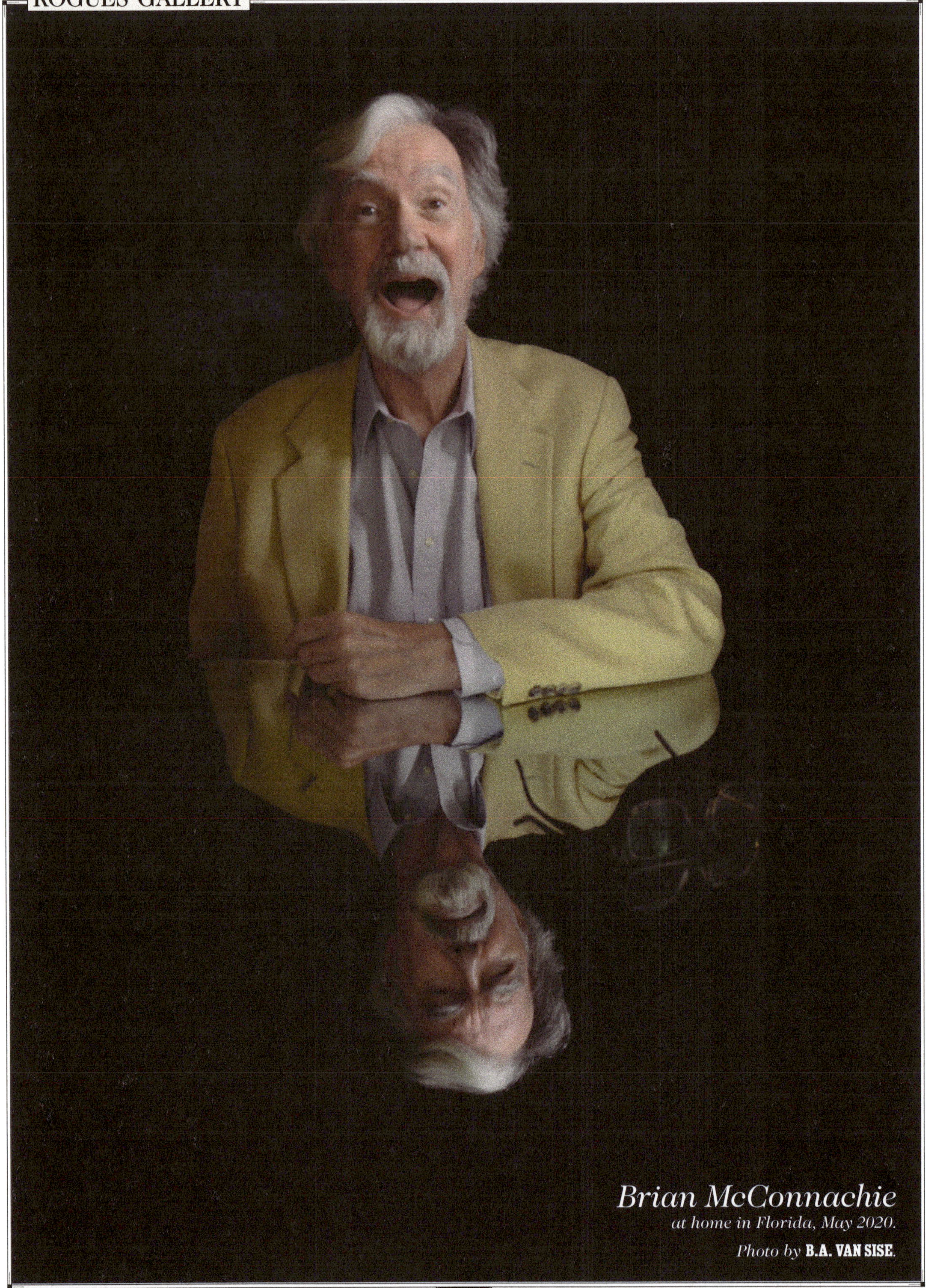

Brian McConnachie
at home in Florida, May 2020.
Photo by **B.A. VAN SISE.**

www.ingramcontent.com/pod-product-compliance
Lightning Source LLC
Chambersburg PA
CBHW061755290426
44108CB00029B/3000